I0438185

Average Doug

My Take on America:
From Politics and Government to Society

Doug Kammerer

iUniverse, Inc.
New York   Bloomington

Average Doug
My Take on America: From Politics and Government to Society

Copyright © 2010 Doug Kammerer

All rights reserved. No part of this book may be used or reproduced by any means, graphic, electronic, or mechanical, including photocopying, recording, taping or by any information storage retrieval system without the written permission of the publisher except in the case of brief quotations embodied in critical articles and reviews.

iUniverse books may be ordered through booksellers or by contacting:

iUniverse
1663 Liberty Drive
Bloomington, IN 47403
www.iuniverse.com
1-800-Authors (1-800-288-4677)

Because of the dynamic nature of the Internet, any Web addresses or links contained in this book may have changed since publication and may no longer be valid. The views expressed in this work are solely those of the author and do not necessarily reflect the views of the publisher, and the publisher hereby disclaims any responsibility for them.

ISBN: 978-1-4401-8952-4 (pbk)
ISBN: 978-1-4401-8953-1 (cloth)
ISBN: 978-1-4401-8951-7 (ebook)

Printed in the United States of America

iUniverse rev. date:2/25/2010-

CONTENTS

ACKNOWLEDGMENTS

I would like to thank the people at iUniverse for helping me with their useful ideas for publishing my book. I would also like to thank my family and friends, who always encouraged me when I wanted to give up.

Introduction

I have always wanted to write a book, but I never knew what type of book I wanted to have published. I thought about both fiction and nonfiction works. Then I thought I would write a book about the state of America today from the viewpoint of a private citizen. After all, I follow politics and current affairs.

I have divided this book into two parts:

- The first part of the book deals with my thoughts on politics and government in America today, including the Fairness Doctrine, government bailouts, and the coming nanny state.
- The second part of the book deals with my thoughts on society today, including how society is rewarding bad behavior and what I would like to tell organizations like NOW and GLAAD.

I am an American citizen who loves his country but doesn't like the direction our country is headed in. This book provides examples of some of the things that are hurting America right now. I never attack anyone personally. I don't call anyone names, and I do not use derogatory language.

PART I

Government and Politics

Chapter 1

My Identity and My Political Philosophy

My name is Douglas Kammerer. I live in northern New Jersey. As far back as I can remember, I have always been interested in American history and politics. In 1984, when President Reagan was running for reelection, I wanted him to win. I became a conservative Republican because of my mom and her side of the family. They believe in less government and more individual freedom. My dad is a Democrat who would often challenge my views in a thoughtful way.

In 1993, when I was sixteen, I decided to volunteer for Christine Todd Whitman's campaign for governor because Governor Florio had raised taxes and hurt the economy. I worked the phone banks, and I felt as if I was helping the campaign. But if I knew then what I know now about how much of a liberal governor she would be and how she would appoint liberals to the state supreme court, I would not have volunteered for her campaign. When she won, I was happy because I felt I had helped.

In 1994 I received two important autographed photos that made me become more of a conservative:

- The first was from Speaker Gingrich. I had written to him when he was house minority whip, thanking him for standing up for conservative values.
- The second was from President Reagan. My mom had received a letter from a friend in California whose husband, a recently retired

3

Secret Service agent, was guarding President Reagan. The letter said I was going to receive an autographed photo from President Reagan. A few weeks later, I did indeed!

In 1995 I went to Adelphi University, where I majored in political science and continued to pursue my interest in government. I still volunteer for political campaigns today. I volunteered for Bret Schundler's gubernatorial campaign in 2001 and always volunteer for Congressman Scott Garrett's campaign when he runs for reelection.

Over the years, because of volunteering and different political events, I have met politicians like Speakers Gingrich and Hastert, Governor Jeb Bush, Governor Romney, Karl Rove, Mayor Giuliani, and Chris Christie, who was elected governor of New Jersey. I have even asked them some important questions. I asked Speaker Gingrich about health care. I asked Governor Romney about immigration. I talked to Chris Christie, and he said he would support Jessica's Law and appoint justices to the state supreme court who were strict constructionists. Also, in 2009 I again worked the phone banks for Chris Christie for governor.

I am proud to say that I am a conservative and strongly believe in the Declaration of Independence, the Constitution, and the Bill of Rights. I also believe that we get our rights from God, not man. I believe that the American people, not the government, know how to spend their money. That is why I am for tax cuts. It is our money, not the government's. I am strongly against redistribution of wealth as well.

I believe that we need lower corporate taxes so business will stay in America and not move overseas because there are fewer taxes and regulations in other countries. When the government cuts taxes, the economy grows, and this helps people. The government does not create jobs; people do. The government can make it easier to create jobs by keeping taxes low or they can make it harder with higher taxes and more regulations.

I also believe that the government is getting too big and intrusive in the lives of the American people. If this continues to happen, people will lose their independence. Then we eventually lose our freedom. I believe that we must have a strong military and national defense or we will become weak. Then terrorists who want to destroy our way of life will attack us.

I believe that, when it comes to health care, the American people should be in charge of their coverage, not the government. We the people know what is best for us, not the government. Do we really want the government in charge of running American's health care? The same government that is bankrupting Social Security, Medicare, and the DMV?

Now people might be saying that I am a Republican, that I agree with everything that Republicans say and can never disagree with Republicans. I am a conservative Republican, but when a Republican says something I disagree with, I am not afraid to say it. I disagreed with McCain/Feingold and the Medicare prescription drug coverage plan. I was against the appointment of Harriet Miers to the U.S. Supreme Court. These are my political views. When I agree or disagree with a politician, I will let people know if he or she is a Republican or a Democrat. When I talk issues, I never disparage anybody that I disagree with. I always respect other people's point of view. After all, if we can't do that, then this isn't America.

Chapter 2

The Bailouts Are Rewarding Failure

Look at companies like Fannie Mae and Freddie Mac that received bailout money. They all committed acts of irresponsible business behavior that have caused these businesses to fail and start to go out of business.

These companies were given bailout money because the government said they were too big to fail. Did they then promise to change the way they operated? No. Only in Washington do we give money to companies on the verge of going under and not get any promises from them to change the way they do business. Some of these companies spent the bailout money on bonuses and fixing up offices. How does that help? Some companies are also asking for more money.

Now look at General Motors and Chrysler. These two companies were on the verge of going under, and they wanted bailout money. Let's look at why they needed all of this bailout money. They needed bailout money because they weren't selling cars. General Motors and Chrysler pleaded, saying that if they didn't get it, they would go under and people would lose jobs. President Bush gave them some bailout money. Now President Obama has given them even more.

General Motors and Chrysler never deserved our taxpayer money, because they haven't promised to change the way their companies are run. Giving them bailout money is like giving money to an alcoholic when he needs it to buy food or clothes and he continues to buy liquor. You wouldn't give an alcoholic money, so why would you want to give these companies money when they won't change the way they run their businesses? It would be better for them to declare bankruptcy and restructure. Declaring bankruptcy is not a bad thing, because you get to start over again.

I keep hearing politicians, including President Obama, say, "These companies are too big to fail," or, "It would be a disaster if these companies go out of business." I disagree. No company is too big to fail. It is sometimes a good thing that a company goes out of business. Then smaller companies who can do a better job take over.

We also now hear that the government wants to buy bad mortgages. This policy again rewards failure. These people were allowed to have mortgages they couldn't afford to pay back. Again, why are the taxpayers going to help these people? What about the people who barely get by and pay their mortgages on time? According to the government, they are screwed for doing the right thing, buying a house they can afford and living within their means.

Here are some additional things to think about. Remember when the tech bubble burst earlier in this decade? Then we had the attacks of 9/11. Then Enron, Global Crossing, and WorldCom collapsed. Many people lost jobs. Retirement plans were ruined. The stock market dropped as well. Did Congress and the Bush administration want to bail out these companies in 2002 and 2003? No. Congress and President Bush did what was right and let the marketplace handle the economy. We need to go back and do what we did in 2003. We should cut taxes and let the mismanaged companies go out of business. The marketplace and capitalism is the best way to solve this crisis.

Chapter 3

There Is Nothing Fair about the Fairness Doctrine

There is nothing fair about the Fairness Doctrine. It is one of those policies that the government creates with good intentions. But it does more harm than good. This doctrine was put in place initially so both sides of an issue could be talked about equally. It was abolished in 1987 under the leadership of President Reagan. Because of this, talk radio was allowed to have any format without having to allow for an alternative viewpoint. When the Fairness Doctrine was law, there was basically no talk radio. If you had a radio show with a conservative viewpoint for two hours, you needed to have a radio show with a liberal viewpoint for two hours for equal time.

Speaker Pelosi wants to bring back the Fairness Doctrine. Although she will never admit it, she wants to silence conservative talk radio. This piece of legislation is unconstitutional. If I own a radio program and I want to have a conservative opinion, I should be allowed. But under the Fairness Doctrine, I would need to have shows with equal points of view. To illustrate my point, let me give you some examples of successful conservative talk radio show hosts who are on the air on weekdays:

Host	Length of Daily Show (Hours)
Rush Limbaugh	3
Sean Hannity	3
Michael Savage	3
Mark Levin	3
Laura Ingraham	3
Glenn Beck	3
Dennis Miller	2
Michael Reagan	3
John Batchelor	4

When we add up all of these hours, the total comes to twenty-seven. Under the Fairness Doctrine, to show balance, I would have to have twenty-seven hours of liberal radio show hosts. There are only twenty-four hours in a day, so in order to comply, I would need to have a conservative day of radio shows and a liberal day of radio shows.

Now let's look at the weekend. The following are some talk show hosts who are on during the weekend:

Host	Length of Daily Show (Hours)
Monica Crowley	3
Larry Kudlow	3
John Batchelor	6

The total comes to twelve hours. So if I owned a radio station, I would need a half-day of conservative talk and a half-day of liberal talk in order to comply. It is ridiculous to think that any radio station would want to pursue any of these ideas. In fact, they will probably start playing music. Notice that when people talk about wanting to bring back the Fairness Doctrine, they only talk about applying it to talk radio. They never talk about bringing it back to television, such as with the network news reports or talk programs.

I believe that conservative talk radio is so successful because no talk show host talks down to his or her audience. They have common sense. They are informative, and you learn something new from them every day. When you listen to talk radio, you actually learn something even if you disagree with the host; they don't make you feel stupid for disagreeing with them.

Liberals actually tried to form their own radio network, called Air America. It had liberals like Senator Al Franken as talk show hosts, but it failed miserably and went bankrupt. So instead of trying to change their format and be successful again, they want to bring back the Fairness Doctrine. Because they cannot succeed in the area of free markets, they want to succeed with government regulation.

For years, conservatives have known that there is a liberal bias in the media. Conservatives never demanded that the Fairness Doctrine return to law and be applied to the evening news to allow for balanced time. Conservatives decided to go on talk radio to get their views heard.

Instead of looking to FOX News and talk radio shows that offer free-market solutions, we should work to solve problems. Liberals look to government to solve this problem by regulating freedom of speech. Liberals should do the same thing and keep working at it instead of trying to destroy the First Amendment. Then they would be doing something smart.

What if the Fairness Doctrine became law? If I buy a conservative newspaper, I must buy a liberal newspaper. If I buy *National Review*, am I going to have to buy a copy of *Nation* magazine to balance it out and be fair? What if I buy a book by a conservative author? Am I going to have to buy a book by a liberal author as well? Is the same thing going to apply when I borrow a library book? This will be the end of free speech. The Fairness Doctrine must never again become law.

When President Reagan, President George H. W. Bush, and President George W. Bush were in office, they never wanted to restore the Fairness Doctrine to be applied to either cable or network news. When Republicans controlled both the House of Representatives and the Senate, no Republican wanted to have the Fairness Doctrine be applied to either cable or network news either. Who really supports free speech? And who doesn't?

What can you, an average citizen, do to stop this?

- Call or write your local congressman. Tell him or her that you are against the Fairness Doctrine because it violates the First Amendment.
- Write a letter to the editor of your local newspaper and express your outrage about Speaker Pelosi wanting to bring back the Fairness Doctrine.
- Tell your friends and family about the Fairness Doctrine. An informed American is the best kind of American. If the American public can be outraged, then the politicians will listen because they want your vote.

Chapter 4

The Coming Nanny State/Socialism to America

The nanny state is when the government arbitrarily decides what's best for us and crams it down our throats after looting our paychecks to pay for it. I am concerned that this country is starting to become a nanny state/socialist country. If this happens, then we will lose our freedom. I want to first talk about the nanny state that is appearing in this country right now.

In New York, New Jersey, and other states, you can no longer smoke in a bar. In New York City, a restaurant cannot serve foods with trans fats[1] in them. The New York City government has even set up a Web site about the trans fats ban. At www.citytech.cuny.edu/notransfatnyc/english/faqs.html, you can see what the city is doing to help businesses. They are giving out pamphlets about the banned trans fats. The ban on trans fats went into effect in July 2008. If you continue to use trans fats after the ban goes into effect, you will be fined between $250 and $2,500. Just imagine if you own a restaurant and now have to worry about the different foods that you serve. If you make unhealthy foods, you can be fined.

You might be thinking that this is good. Both smoking and fatty foods are bad for you. But this is not good, because the government is telling people what kind of restaurant atmosphere they can have and what kind of food they can serve. If someone wants to open a bar and

---

1   A trans fat is an oil that is added to foods to make them taste better.

wants to allow smoking in it, he or she should be allowed to do so. The same goes for someone who wants to open a bar that does not allow smoking. Also, if someone wants to open a restaurant that serves fried foods, he or she should have the right to do so. The same goes for someone who wants to open a healthy restaurant. Nobody is forcing anybody to go to a bar with smoking; nobody is forcing people to eat foods that are high in fat. People should be able to choose what they want without the government involved.

If the government can keep people from smoking in bars and from trans fats in food, what else is next? Will they decide to ban red meat because they say that too much red meat is bad for you? Will they ban ice cream because too much ice cream can be bad for you? How about fried foods? I have heard that too much food is bad for you. Will the government say that fat people can't eat certain foods because they are unhealthy for them?

Could the government ban personal behavior as well? Certain things can be dangerous, like football, soccer, baseball, hiking, camping, mountain climbing, dirt-bike racing, swimming, diving, basketball, and running. After a while, it gets ridiculous to think about. When you are a child, you enjoy swimming. When I was young I went to the swimming pool and had a lot of fun going off the high dive. I also enjoyed playing baseball, running around, and playing outside with friends. Imagine when children can't use a diving board, go down a waterslide at a pool, or play sports. What kind of childhood would it be? I think it would be boring. Basically, there would be no childhood.

I know what you are thinking: "Don't be silly! The government won't go that far!" But who would have thought that the government would ban trans fats or two teenagers would sue McDonald's for making them fat? But that's what has happened.

When the government bans something, they take away our freedom and damage the marketplace as well. For example, consider the pool hall called High Pockets, one of the most successful pool halls in America. When the Westchester County government decided to ban smoking in bars and restaurants, High Pockets went out of business because of this ban.

Some people actually want the government to become a nanny state. Morgan Spurlock directed and starred in the documentary *Super*

Size Me. He was only going to eat at McDonald's for a month and not exercise. Both my mom and I thought, "What an idiot!" He had all of these health problems because he was eating McDonald's food all the time. Why would he do such a dumb thing? Eating at McDonald's for thirty days isn't good for you. Anybody could tell you that.

So I decided to watch the movie one day. I didn't like it at all. First, Morgan Spurlock didn't do something courageous by eating at McDonald's for a month and risking his health. He should have known that this diet was going to hurt him. At the end of his movie, he says that he wants McDonald's to expand their menu because he doesn't want to choose between extra large and extra large food.

I have a few ideas for stupid topics for movies. How about a movie about how bad cigarettes are? I could smoke two cartons of cigarettes for thirty days. During the same time, we could look at how my health deteriorates the way that Morgan Spurlock's did in *Super Size Me.* Why don't I drink two bottles of Scotch for thirty days and see how much my health deteriorates as well? Those two ideas for movies are ridiculous. Of course my health would deteriorate. Anybody would know that. I would be an idiot for risking my health for such a stupid reason.

Then Morgan Spurlock wrote *Don't Eat This Book,* where he says he doesn't want litigation. He wants lawmakers to change laws against restaurants and others. I have a better solution for him and others who hate McDonald's and want Americans to become healthier. Instead of wanting to ban people from going to McDonald's, why not open a chain of healthy restaurants? This is a better solution than making a movie about McDonald's and how eating too much is bad for you. You would be using the free marketplace to help an idea that could really catch on. That is the American way. If Morgan Spurlock had done a movie about wanting to open a healthy fast-food restaurant, I would have more respect for him.

The Center for Science in the Public Interest really pushes for the nanny state. They say you shouldn't eat fettuccine alfredo because it is extremely unhealthy. These people seem to complain when a fast-food restaurant adds something new to the menu that isn't good for you. All they want to do is have the government control every aspect of society.

Michael Bloomberg, the mayor of New York City, is the "king of the nanny state." Since becoming mayor, he banned smoking in bars and restaurants before the entire state decided to. Then he banned trans fats in foods served in restaurants and in other foods as well. He also wants a high commuter tax because he wants New York City to go green. A so-called commuter tax will not make the environment cleaner. In fact, it will only hurt the poor and middle class who go into the city to work every day. If Mayor Bloomberg wanted to make the air cleaner, he would lower fares on buses and subways.

Mayor Bloomberg thinks that he is better and smarter than the voters of New York City are. Because of the latest economic crisis and other budgetary crises, he has basically decided that only he can solve the problems of New York City. So he went to the city council and asked them to repeal the two-term limit and change it to three. Despite the fact that the voters have passed the two-term limit numerous times, with a large number of voters backing it, the city council granted his request so he could run again.

Mayor Bloomberg won a third term. Now what will he want to pass in New York City to make it more of a nanny state? Will he raise parking meter fees so people won't drive their cars into the city? Will he outlaw sugar because eating too much sugar will make you fat? We should just get ready for even more nanny-state laws in New York City.

President Obama wants America to become a socialist country. Joe Wurzelbacher (Joe the Plumber) asked President Obama about his tax plan and how it would hurt him. Joe was going to start a new business where he would be making between $250,000 and $300,000 a year. President Obama responded that he wanted to spread the wealth around. He also says that when you cut taxes from the bottom up, everyone benefits. If President Obama really cared about wealth, he would have said that he wants to make it easier to create wealth.

President Obama is also making America a socialist country by becoming involved with American business. He fired Rick Wagoner, the CEO of General Motors. Then he bailed out GM because he said these companies are too big to fail. He is proposing legislation called cap and trade. This legislation is supposed to lower carbon emissions by allowing companies to buy carbon credits. If companies go over their allotment of credits, they will be fined. This legislation will not reduce carbon emissions at all but is another tax that will hurt businesses, consumers, and households. He is also trying to have government-run health care, proposing legislation that will add a public option to health insurance.

Also consider all of President Obama's government czars. The green jobs czar, Van Jones, is a known Communist. In "Will a Red Help Blacks Go Green?" Aaron Klein states that Van Jones has radical ties. According to this article, "He sees his environmental activism as a means to fight for social justice and class justice." Also, we learn from the article that Van Jones was arrested after the Rodney King verdict, and after his arrest he became a Communist. Fortunately for America Van Jones no longer works in the White House. However, there are still plenty of other radicals who work as czars in the administration. Then there is Mark Lloyd, who gave a speech at a Market for Media Reform conference. In the speech he praised Venezuelan president Hugo Chavez and the way that he took control of the media. Also consider White House communications czar Anita Dunn, who said in a graduation speech in 2009 that Mao Tse Tung is someone she admires. Then there is regulatory czar Cass Sunstein. He is someone who wants to give animals the rights to sue people in court. Next there is manufacturing czar Ron Bloom, who in a speech at the Sixth Annual Distressed Investing Forum at the Union League Club in New York in February 2008 said, "We know the joke that the free market place is a job." Then he goes on to say, "We kinda agree with Mao that political power comes from a barrel of a gun."

Now things might sound grim, but that doesn't mean that we Americans should give up. We need to take action. We need to write to our congressmen and tell him or her that we don't want America to become a nanny state/socialist country. This has worked before. In the early 1990s, when President Clinton was pushing "HillaryCare," Americans found out about the plan and wrote their congressmen to tell them not to support this legislation. It worked. "HillaryCare" never became law. Then it worked again in 2007 when it came to the McCain/Kennedy bill, an immigration reform bill that would grant amnesty to illegal immigrants living in America. When people found out about this bill, they contacted their congressmen to oppose this legislation.

Because of this, McCain/Kennedy was stopped from becoming law. We also must work twice as hard because the Pelosi health-care bill has passed the House of Representatives. It faces an uncertain fate in the Senate. However, we must contact our U.S. senators and tell them that we don't want the government running our health care. Also visit DickMorris.com; we need to help in his efforts to stop government-run health care. Next year is the 2010 midterm election. If you live in a state that has a senator who is up for reelection you must contact your senator and tell him or her that you don't support government-run health care and that you will not vote for them if they support government-run health care. Again this bill can and must be defeated. We must not back down from this fight for one moment. The other side will be backing down next. They will do everything they can to pass health-care reform, even going so far as to break campaign promises of posting bills on line seventy-two hours before they are voted on so the general public can read them, or not even reading the bill that they write until after the bill is passed, and even passing bills in the dead of night. We need to keep fighting, because our freedom depends on it.

Chapter 5

Health-Care Reform

If you were to listen to President Obama, Nancy Pelosi, Harry Reid, and the rest of the Democrats in Congress you would think that our health-care system is the worst in the world and that if we don't pass their health-care bill, which has a government option, tomorrow, our health-care system will fail. I am here to tell you that this is a lie and that the real reason they want health-care reform passed quickly is because they know that the American people don't want it because it is too expensive and will lead to higher taxes and more government control of the economy.

America has the best health-care system in the entire world. Our hospitals are the best. If you get sick in America, whether you have cancer or need bypass surgery, you will see a doctor and get the appropriate surgery right away. Even if you don't have health insurance you can still go to an emergency room and get treated for your illness. What we need in America is not health-care reform but insurance reform. If we get insurance reform that will make our health-care system better than what it is now. I have to warn you about something. The same people who want the government option to become part of health care won't come out and say it. So they go around and say, "We want competition and choice." Don't be fooled, because if there is any type of government option there will be no choice and competition.

Yet we constantly hear about the need to pass health-care reform because the insurance companies are greedy and want to make a profit.

We hear that we need a public option, which should be called the government option because the government will be in charge of your health care. This means that the same government that runs Social Security and Medicare will decide your health care. What is also something of concern is that the same people who want to pass health-care reform don't want to debate it. They won't even allow the bill to be posted online so the American public can read it.

If this health-care bill is passed with the government option it will ruin our health-care system. It will lead to longer lines to see a doctor and get treatment for whatever is bothering us. Basically our health-care system will become what is in Great Britain. If you don't believe me just go to youtube.com and listen to British member of Parliament Daniel Hannon. He has spoken out against the British health-care system, warning America not to have nationalized health care.

Now if the government asked me for my opinion on health care this is what I would tell them that they need to do: tell the truth about the debate on health-care reform. We don't need health-care reform; we need insurance reform. Second, we need to have lawsuit reform. Part of the reason why insurance premiums are rising is because of lawsuits. We need to make insurance easier to buy. Here are two options that would work to expand insurance coverage: First, we can set up either medical saving accounts or tax credits for people who can't afford health insurance. Second, we can make buying health insurance a similar process to buying car insurance. When you have health insurance you can only have health insurance from the state that you live in; however, when you buy car insurance you can buy it from a company in a different state. Also, we should allow people who move from one state to another to keep their health insurance. We can also establish with little government action that if something is in an insurance policy it must be followed, and they must cover someone with a preexisting condition. This would be easy to ensure by giving insurance companies tax breaks. If these reforms are set up it will be a big step toward lowering health-care premiums and costs because people will be able to negotiate what type of coverage they want. By doing this, more people will have health insurance.

Finally, we can't have Obama care. This will lead to America having a European type of health care. Under this type of health care we will have the government in charge. Think about it. The same government that is having problems and having shortages with the H1N1 flu vaccine will now be in charge of running the health-care system. That is why we need to continue to rally and tell our congressmen and senators that we don't want our health care taken away.

Chapter 6

Whatever Happened to Lindsey Graham?

Senator Lindsey Graham was elected to Congress as part of the Republican Revolution in 1994. When he was first in the House of Representatives he was a small-government conservative who supported tax cuts, increased defense spending, and less government. In fact, in 1998 he helped to lead the effort to impeach President Clinton. He was also a house manager during the Senate trial of President Clinton. But somewhere between then and now Lindsey Graham has become a member of the Washington establishment and has forgotten about the people who elected him to Congress.

In 2002 Lindsey Graham was elected to the U.S. Senate. Now that he is in the Senate he has become more liberal and has started to support legislation sponsored by Senator John McCain. Just as Senator McCain does he always tries to hurt conservatives and compromise with Democrats on every issue. For example in 2005 when Republican Senate leaders were trying to stop Senate Democrats filibustering with the nuclear option, Lindsey Graham was a part of the gang of fourteen who led a compromise to stop the filibuster on certain Bush judicial nominees; future nominees could be filibustered only for extraordinary reasons. In 2007 he was a supporter of a McCain/Kennedy immigration reform bill that would give amnesty to illegal immigrants. When this legislation was blocked in the Senate because the American people didn't want it to become law, he blamed the Republicans and talk radio for it not becoming law. In the 2008 election he was a backer of

Senator John McCain and criticized conservatives who had a hard time supporting Senator McCain.

In 2009, when Senator Specter left the GOP because he was facing a Senate primary challenge against former senator Pat Toomey that he was going to lose, Senator Graham was on Greta Van Susteren's show *On the Record*. While on the show he blamed Republicans for Senator Specter's defection to the Democrats, basically saying "Republicans are forcing out moderates." Then he attacked Pat Toomey and Republicans in Pennsylvania for having the nerve to hold a primary against Senator Specter. He also told Pat Toomey that he couldn't win in Pennsylvania because he was too conservative and that he was going to try to get former Homeland Security secretary Tom Ridge, also a former governor of Pennsylvania, to run against Senator Specter in the election next year.

If I could tell Senator Graham something, this is what I would tell him. I would say what happened to you? When you were first a member of the House you were a conservative. Now you are nothing but a liberal who is part of the establishment in Washington. You don't represent the people of South Carolina. Instead you represent Washington DC. It is an outrage that you would blame Republicans and talk radio for McCain/Kennedy not being passed. The American people called and faxed their congressmen and senators and did not want this legislation to become law. Also, how dare you tell Pat Toomey that he can't win in Pennsylvania; conservatives can win there. Do you remember Senator Rick Santorum? He is just as conservative as Pat Toomey, and he was elected there twice. In fact, the reason why he lost there in 2006 was because it was an anti-Republican year.

I would tell Senate Graham that cap and trade is a lousy idea that won't reduce greenhouse gases. All it will do is raise taxes on households and businesses that can't afford it. It will help out foreign countries because corporations will send jobs overseas where there are no cap and trade laws, so Americans will lose jobs. Also, your idea that it will lead to less war is the stupidest idea that I have ever heard. If you want something right why don't you stand up for the people of South Carolina and not for the Washington elite? If you do this Republicans and especially conservatives will respect you again.

My concluding thought about Lindsey Graham is this: we don't need him in the Republican Party. He is trying to be just like Senator McCain before he got the Republican nomination in 2008 and wants to be loved by the press and the liberal establishment. So to get their love he will attack regular Americans and people who disagree with his ideas. If Republicans listen to Lindsey Graham they will lose elections.

Chapter 7

How the Courts Are Becoming Legislatures

If you look at a copy of the U.S. Constitution, you will see the articles about the legislative, executive, and judicial branches. Unfortunately, the judicial branch is now starting to take over more in deciding the role of Americans. The founding fathers never wanted this to happen. In fact, if they had any inkling about this happening, they would have done more to limit the powers of the judicial branch. Look at some of the ways that an active judicial branch has taken away the rights of Americans and given rights to people who shouldn't have additional rights:

- *Kelo v. New London*
  This case dealt with eminent domain abuse. The Supreme Court said that local government could take your property, such as your home or business, if it would help the government receive more revenue. This is an outrage. Property rights have just gone out the window.
- *Boumediene v. Bush*
  This case allows detainees at Guantanamo Bay to challenge their status as enemy combatants. If you are fighting against our troops and you are caught, you can now appeal in American civilian courts. The people who are caught on the battlefield are not criminals. They are terrorists fighting in a war trying to kill American soldiers. This ruling is extremely dangerous. When they appeal their status

in our courts, terror suspects will be talking to lawyers. They will definitely try to use their lawyers to give information to other terrorists. Lynne Stewart was taking information from her client, Sheikh Abdel-Rahman. If it happened once, it will happen again. Also, if they get released on bond, these terror suspects will be out on the streets of American.

Consider these other outrages by state supreme courts:

- The high court in Massachusetts ruled in a decision that allowed gays to marry. Where in the state's constitution does it allow this?
- The California State Supreme Court overturned a ban on gay marriage that was passed by the voters of California. Then the voters in California went to the polls in November 2008 and passed Proposition 208, which amended the state constitution to ban gay marriage. The matter went to the state supreme court because gay rights groups said the amendment was unconstitutional. The California Supreme Court said that Proposition 208 was constitutional, though homosexuals married before Prop 208 became law were still legally married.
- The New Jersey Supreme Court decided to rewrite election law in 2002. In early October 2002, Doug Forrester was leading Senator Bob Torricelli by twelve points. Torricelli dropped out of the Senate race after the state legislature said you could replace a candidate, but the state's Democrats sued to have former senator Lautenberg's name put on the ballot. The state's supreme court agreed unanimously, despite what the law had said.

The Ninth Circuit Court of Appeals has to be the most leftist court in America. This court has the highest turnover rate in the Supreme Court as well. For instance, this court said that "one nation under God," as said in the Pledge of Allegiance, is unconstitutional. The U.S. Supreme Court overturned this ruling on a technicality, but I'm not saying that someone won't try this again.

A judge's job is not to be a legislator. Chief Justice John Roberts said about judges, "They are supposed to be an umpire when it comes to the law." I agree. Judges are supposed to see if there are laws that are abusing or taking away people's rights. They were never supposed to legislate from the bench. It is extremely dangerous for a judge to act as if he or she is a legislator. Just because a judge wears a black robe and is called "Your Honor," this doesn't make him or her a king or queen. It doesn't mean that he or she can make up laws.

Some justices on the U.S. Supreme Court want to use international laws to decide Supreme Court rulings in the United States. This is just as outrageous as a judge legislating from the bench. They are breaking the oath that they swore to uphold when they became a justice, which is to protect and defend the U.S. Constitution. Justices Ginsberg, Breyer, Stevens, and O'Connor have all given speeches about how the United States must use foreign law when writing opinions for the Supreme Court. Justice Kennedy used foreign law to decide *Lawrence v. Texas,* in which the European Court on Human Rights was quoted.

This is not what justices are supposed to do. They are not supposed to rely on foreign law. Are they going to rely on sharia law next? In my opinion, justices who rely on foreign law should be impeached. They are breaking their oath to protect and defend the U.S. Constitution. Any lawyer who wants American courts to look to foreign law should not become a judge in this country.

The president appoints judges to the federal courts system; governors appoint judges in some states. So ask candidates who run for president or governor, "What kind of justices will you appoint to the benches? Will you appoint strict constructionists who will not rewrite laws?" Also, state and federal senators vote to confirm these judges, so ask these candidates, "If you are elected, what kind of justices will you vote for?" In some states, justices run for office. If you live in a state where you can vote for a justice, ask, "What kind of justice will you be? Will you be a justice who will be a constructionist? Will you be a justice who will legislate from the bench?"

In the spring of 2009, Justice David Souter announced that he was retiring from the U.S. Supreme Court. This gave President Obama an opportunity to replace him, so he named Sonia Sotomayor, a justice on the Second Court of Appeals. I would oppose her nomination to the Supreme Court because of how she feels about her role as a judge. She has said, "Court of Appeals is where policy is made." As a justice and member of the Supreme Court, she will try to be a judicial activist and make policy.

Chapter 8

Thank You, Arlen Specter

I want to thank the one person who is responsible for two of the Supreme Court decisions that took away our rights as American citizens. Senator Arlen Specter always does what he thinks is best for himself. For years, he was a Republican in name only. Instead of helping the Republicans, he would rather support the Democrats and have the media and Washington elite like him.

In 1987, President Reagan nominated Robert Bork to the Supreme Court. Senator Ted Kennedy said that "although the judge had abandoned his most Neanderthal views, his appointment would result in an America where women would be forced into back alley abortions, blacks would sit at segregated lunch counters, and rogue police would break down citizens' doors."[2]

Senator Kennedy attacked Robert Bork on nothing but lies, and Senator Specter supported Senator Kennedy by being one of the first senators to say he was going to oppose Robert Bork. Because of Senator Specter's efforts, Robert Bork's nomination to the Supreme Court was defeated.

President Reagan then decided to nominate Douglas Ginsburg. But Ginsburg soon withdrew his nomination. So President Reagan nominated Anthony Kennedy, who has turned out to be a swing vote on the Supreme Court. Some of his decisions have been extremely

---

2   "Ted Kennedy Speech on Senate Floor," *New York Times* July 3, 1987.

harmful to America. Two of the worst Supreme Court discussions can be blamed on him: *Kelo v. New London* and *Boumediene v. Bush*.

If Robert Bork had been on the Supreme Court, he would have voted with Chief Justice Rehnquist and justices Thomas, Scalia, and O'Connor in *Kelo v. New London*. I wish no personal harm to Senator Specter. I wonder how he would feel if his home or business were taken away because the government wanted more money and could give away his land to a huge business.

I would also like to thank Senator Specter for *Boumediene v. Bush*. Senator Specter's role in this case again goes back to the Robert Bork confirmation. If Robert Bork had been confirmed, the case would have gone five to four the other way, and detainees at Guantanamo Bay would not have had the right to sue in federal court about their detainee status.

In 1986, Senator Specter voted to confirm William Rehnquist as chief justice. He also voted to confirm Antonin Scalia to become an associate justice on the court. Associate Justice Scalia and Robert Bork basically had the same judicial philosophy, yet Senator Specter voted to confirm Scalia. I wonder if Senator Specter was faking his vote for Scalia or if he voted against Bork because he wanted the media elites to like him. Whatever the case, it is disgraceful that Senator Specter voted for Associate Justice Scalia and against Robert Bork. Another consequence of Senator Specter's voting against Justice Bork is that in 1990 when Justice William J. Brennen Jr. retired there was a golden opportunity for President George H. W. Bush to nominate a conservative to the Supreme Court. However, President Bush didn't want to nominate someone with a long paper trail because of what had happened three years earlier with Justice Bork's nomination. So he nominated a stealth conservative, David Souter. Many people were surprised by David Souter's nomination because few people outside of New Hampshire knew who he was. Justice Souter ended up disappointing conservatives because he became one of the Supreme Court's liberal members. If Justice Bork had been confirmed Justice Souter probably would not have been nominated to the U.S. Supreme Court.

Here are a few things to do about Senator Specter:

• Write to Senator Specter and tell him how you feel.

- If you live in Pennsylvania, you can vote against him in 2010. In 2004, he almost lost in the Republican primary to former congressman Pat Toomey. Now Senator Specter has decided to become a Democrat because he will lose the Republican primary to Pat Toomey. I say, "Good-bye, Senator Specter. You were never a Republican, and we won't miss you at all."

Chapter 9

If Liberals Could Rewrite the Constitution

If liberals had their way and were able to write the U.S. Constitution and Bill of Rights today, some rights would not be there, and certain rights would be added. The Constitution would not say "We the People." It would say "The government of the United States." Both the executive and judicial branches would probably be stronger as well based on the following:

- The president would have a line-item veto and more input on legislation than he does right now.
- The judicial branch would be given more power to strike down laws and rewrite laws more easily.
- There would no electoral college. Presidential candidates would only go to California, Texas, New York, and Florida to campaign instead of other states.
- There would be a greater chance of voter fraud. Instead of focusing on both big and small states to get to the total of 270 electoral votes, presidential candidates would focus solely on large states with big cities like New York, California, Texas, Illinois, and Florida, and there would be a greater chance of voter fraud and misrepresentation.
- Government-run health care would be a right.

I really want to focus on the Bill of Rights because I feel that if it were written today it would be completely different:

- Under the new First Amendment:
- Congress would still have freedom of religion, but there would be a separation of church and state.
- Our freedom of speech would be limited, saying one could not say anything offensive to anyone.
- The Fairness Doctrine would be included.
- The right to privacy would be included.
- The Second Amendment, the right to keep and bear arms, would be rewritten or not exist at all.
- The Eighth Amendment would be expanded to include terrorists and would set strict guidelines about interrogating a suspected criminal.
- The Tenth Amendment would be completely rewritten, giving more power to the federal government and less power to the states and people.

The U.S. Constitution is not going to be rewritten. But we need to be on guard against little changes that affect our freedoms, such as the McCain/Feingold law that limits political freedom of speech. Another example is the bailouts. Are they constitutional? The government is taking over private industries, and they are also dictating the pay of CEOs. Then there is the health-care bill that Congress is trying to pass. Again, how is that constitutional? The government is going to be dictating to insurance companies and telling doctors what to do and will again be taking over and running the economy. That is why we need to guard against lawmakers who want to have government take over everything because it is helping people. Only these lawmakers aren't helping people; instead they are taking away more of our freedoms. Also, what if liberal justices strike down laws they don't like or expand the Constitution? Or what if these same liberal justices decide to give new rights to people because they want to? We must be on guard against people who say the Constitution is a living, breathing document, because it isn't. It is the foundation of the way our country works.

Chapter 10

Questions I Would Ask President Obama, and My Advice to Him

If I had a chance to question President Obama, I would ask him the following serious questions about American foreign policy, America as a country, taxes, health care, security issues, and so forth.

- Why do you feel that this stimulus package will work with all of this government spending? When will this spending stop?
- If more companies ask for government bailout money, will you give it to them?
- You continue to talk about taxing the rich. How do you personally feel about the rich?
- Are you going to cut defense spending in order to pay for these new government programs, or are you going to cut other wasteful spending?
- When you were a state senator in 2001 you gave an interview to Chicago radio station WBEZ.FM where you said that the success of the civil rights movement was in people being given rights and you being able to sit at a lunch counter if able to pay for your meal. You said that the Supreme Court never ventured into the redistribution of wealth and economic justice in society. Also, you said that the Warren Court was not that radical and didn't break free from the constraints of the founding fathers and the Constitution. You also went on to say that the Constitution is a charter of negative

liberties. Do you still feel this way about the Supreme Court and the Warren Court?

- What is your opinion of the founding fathers?
- How do you personally feel about the military?
- Do you think that your cap-and-trade legislation will hurt American businesses?
- Why did you feel it necessary to fire the CEO of General Motors? What gives you the power to do so?
- In a CNN debate in the summer of 2007, you responded to a question about unconditionally meeting with the leaders of Iran, North Korea, Cuba, and Venezuela. You said that you would have also called these countries "little countries." Since these comments, you have backed off from meeting with these leaders. When will you meet with them?
- Why did you decide to close Guantanamo Bay? Where are you going to put these prisoners on American soil?
- Why did you release some interrogation techniques to the media? Do you feel that the techniques are torture?
- By releasing the interrogation techniques to the media, do you think you have weakened national security?
- Do you feel that America is an arrogant country? If so, give examples.
- Why do you want a government option in health care, such as in Canada and Great Britain, which will lead to more lines and longer waits to see a doctor? Also, have you heard any of the warnings to America not to have government-run health care, such as from Great Britain by British Parliament member Daniel Hannon?
- Instead of reforming our health-care system, why not reform our insurance industry to make it easier for people to buy their insurance?
- Why are you attacking FOX News?
- Why are you willing to meet with dictators like Hugo Chavez, Daniel Ortega, and Kim Jong-Il, and yet you won't go on FOX News?
- Did you know that Van Jones was a Communist and that Anita Dunn has said that Mao Zedong is someone she admires, as Cass Sunstein has also stated? Also, what is your opinion of Mao Zedong?

- In the last question in your press conference in July 2009, you commented on the arrest of your friend Henry Louis Gates. "I don't know the facts, but the police acted stupidly." Why did you comment on the case without knowing all of the facts? How do you personally feel about law enforcement in America?
- Also, when the attack on Fort Hood happened you didn't want to comment without knowing all the facts, yet you didn't know all the facts in the Henry Louis Gates case and you commented on it. Why is that?

  These questions are fair and important. Americans need to know:
- If the president will continue to spend money to help the economy
- If the president will give out more bailout money to companies if they ask for it
- Why the president fired the CEO of General Motors and what gives him the power to do so
- How the president feels about America

I would advise President Obama to read the 9/11 Commission Report. In the report, it says that al Qaeda and other terrorists were at war before we were. When he makes a speech, he should not blame the previous administration for what is happening in America now. It will eventually get old. I would also tell him, "Who cares what the UN or European elite think about America? You should have a foreign policy that is only in America's best interest." By doing this, he will protect America and promote freedom in the world.

I would also advise the president that when it comes to FOX News don't act childish; go on their network for interviews. Just because they are being fair and balanced in their news coverage that doesn't make them any less of a news outlet. MSNBC shows nothing but favorable coverage of you, and they are considered a news outlet. Also, President Bush was hammered constantly by MSNBC, CBS, CNN, and ABC because he was a conservative. Yet he and his administration never declared war on any of these networks. Neither Karl Rove nor any other member of his administration ever went on network news show and attacked any news network. His press secretaries always took questions from their reporters. David Gregory, who constantly criticized President Bush, was called on at press conferences. The president appeared on

NBC's *Meet the Press* and was interviewed by Tom Brokaw. My final point about the boycott of FOX News is that it is dangerous because presidents of the United States are not supposed to control the First Amendment. No other president has ever done this.

Finally I would tell him this about the situation in Afghanistan: Do what is best for the troops. Stop capitulating about it. General McChrystal, the person you appointed to lead the fight in Afghanistan, needs more troops. Send him the troops that he needs. You have had his report since August requesting more troops. Every day that you wait and don't make up your mind you are making America look weak and indecisive to the world. Send the troops that General McChrystal needs to win in Afghanistan. If you don't, the war in Afghanistan will continue to get worse and more Americans soldiers will continue to die. Because you haven't sent in the recommended troops, October 2009 was one of the bloodiest months in Afghanistan. Also, don't compromise and send in fewer troops to try and satisfy the Left in America. If you do this you will continue to put American troops in danger, and America will not be fighting at full strength. If Afghanistan continues to become worse and the Taliban are allowed to take over again, al Qaeda will once again rebuild their terrorist bases in Afghanistan and will gain confidence and once again be able to attack America like they did in the attack on the USS *Cole*. If that happens you can bet there will be another 9/11 attack on America, and nobody wants that. So, President Obama, do the right thing and send the troops that General McChrystal needs.

Chapter 11

President Obama Knows What He Is Doing

President Obama knows what he is doing. All you need to do is look at what he has said during the campaign. Also, just look at the background of the czars that President Obama has appointed to his administration, and look at how the White House has felt about them as well. Look at the war on FOX News and you will see that President Obama knows exactly what he is doing.

When President Obama was running for president he always talked about changing America. In fact, on October 30, 2008, at a speech at the University of Missouri he said, "We are five days away from fundamentally changing America." If you think about that line, notice that he didn't say that we are five days away from winning or that we are five days away from putting America back on the right course.

Also, look at the people whom President Obama has appointed to work for him in his administration. The first person he picked was Rahm Emanuel as his White House chief of staff. Rahm Emanuel used to represent Congressman Dan Rostenkowski's congressional district. I met him twice, and he was extremely arrogant. Look at the different czars whom the White House has appointed. Some people were shocked to learn that green jobs czar Van Jones was a Communist. Some in the media thought that the White House must not have done a good job with its vetting process. However, if we simply look at Obama aide Valerie Jarrett answering a question about Van Jones at the Netroot Nation Convention, she speaks glowingly of Van Jones and says how the White House is so happy to finally have him in the administration. Then she goes on to say that they have been following his career for a long time. If we look at that statement we can believe that President Obama knows the background of his czars. I believe this to be the case of all of his other czars as well.

I also believe that President Obama knows exactly what he is doing with the war against FOX News. President Obama has had great press coverage, especially when it comes to MSNBC news, which has news anchors like Chris Matthews who said on the air about President Obama that when he speaks, "I get a thrill up my leg." I will discuss FOX News in more depth later in this book, but I want to say that President Obama doesn't like the fact that FOX News doesn't fawn over him. He gets treated fairly. They don't favor him, and they criticize him. So President Obama and Rahm Emanuel decided to declare war on FOX News. The reason they are doing this is because they want to distract the media by talking about FOX News so they can also distract the American people and possibly pass health care or cap and trade or get away with continuing to appoint left-wing radicals in the administration.

I know that Attorney General Eric Holder wants to investigate alleged torture abuses by the CIA. While I believe that he wants to do this, President Obama has spoken out against the CIA being investigated for alleged torture. I believe that President Obama believes that the CIA has tortured terror suspects and wants them investigated, because he could have called up the attorney general, Eric Holder, and told him not to investigate the CIA. By not stopping the investigation of the CIA I believe that President Obama wants it to happen.

I also think that President Obama still believes what he said about income distribution and the Supreme Court in 2001. Just look at his nomination as regulatory czar and how he is now trying to dictate CEO pay. Also look at who he has nominated to the Supreme Court. Because of his statements on income distribution I think that President Obama is not a fan of capitalism, and that is why he wants to pass health care and cap and trade. If President Obama really supported capitalism he would be against cap and trade and would look to the free market to stop pollution and reform health care.

Also remember when President Obama spoke out against the cops in the Henry Louis Gates case without knowing all the facts. I believe that President Obama wanted to comment on the case, and that is why he asked that reporter to question him about it at his press conference in July. Also, President Obama not wanting to comment on the Ft. Hood shooting without all the facts happened because he was being politically correct. Now look at President Obama on the war on terror. He signed a bill that was written by Senator Ted Kennedy that made 9/11 a day of volunteering. Also, President Obama doesn't use the term *war on terror* anymore. There is a reason why he is doing this; I believe because he doesn't agree with America on this issue. I also believe that the reason why President Obama is taking a long time in deciding whether to send in the recommended troops to Afghanistan is because he and his base don't really want to fight the war there either. During the presidential election President Obama firmly voiced that he opposed the war in Iraq. He kept saying that we took our eye off of Afghanistan. Now that he is president and he can doing something in Afghanistan he doesn't know if he really wants to fight there or not, and he is trying to get the support of his left-wing base. Also, President Obama has decided not to attend the twentieth-anniversary celebration of the fall of the Berlin Wall. The reason why I believe that he has decided not to attend the celebration is simple—we need to look at what he said when he visited France this year. Remember he said that America had at times acted arrogantly. So I believe that President Obama is not showing up because he doesn't want an American presence during this celebration.

President Obama in the third presidential debate against Senator McCain gave examples of both Democrats and Republicans whom he would associate with to get policy advice. One example, on economic advice, would be Warren Buffett and former Federal Reserve chairman Paul Volker. So if I were to judge the president by the statement that he said above, I would now look at President Obama and the people that he has surrounded himself with, like Reverend Jeremiah Wright for twenty years, and his sitting on a board with Bill Ayers and having a fundraiser in his house when he first ran for office. President Obama thinks that America has done more harm than good in the world, that basically it is an evil country. Then if we look at the czars mentioned earlier whom President Obama has working in his administration we see that he supports what Hugo Chavez has done in Venezuela in cracking down on freedom of speech, and he might want to do this in America. Again, look at the czars whom he has appointed. If we look at what they have said we know that President Obama doesn't like the free market and wants to redistribute wealth.

We must also look at what President Obama has said in the past about this. If we look at his past statements to form our opinion of President Obama we can conclude that President Obama wants to redistribute wealth, that he does not have a favorable view of the founding fathers, and that he thinks that the Constitution and the Bill of Rights are negative freedoms.

In conclusion, all we need to remember about President Obama is that he knows what he is doing. We know that President Obama is trying to attack people who disagree with him on issues because he has taken positions that I have mentioned in earlier chapters that are left-of-center. Again, these are my opinions about President Obama. I am only doing what he told us to do, and that is to judge him by the people that he has surrounded himself with in the White House, and I am judging him by statements that he has made in the past. By the way, he has never disavowed these statements either during the presidential campaign or as president. Also, I am judging him by statements that he has made as president. By doing this I believe that we can get a better understanding of who President Obama is and what he wants to do to America.

Chapter 12

Criticizing President Obama

From what you have read you don't have to guess that I am not a fan of President Obama or his policies. You would be right on that. I think that President Obama's policies are harmful to the country. I think that they will make America a socialist country, and I don't want that to happen. But does this mean that I am a racist? No it doesn't.

I hate the way the liberals in the media and in Hollywood are saying that if you disagree with President Obama you are a racist. Notice that when African Americans like Reverend Jesse Jackson and Al Sharpton disagreed with President Bush it was never said that they were racists because they disagreed with him. I never thought that either. For the media and other liberal and left-wing people to say this is simpleminded and in a way racist. For America to elect an African American president proves just how great this country is. To be able to criticize him for his policies again shows how great America is. If President Obama decides to listen to the advice of General McChrystal and decides to send him the forty thousand troops that he needs to fight in Afghanistan, I would support him on this issue. However, when he decides to support a health-care system that will have the government taking it over I don't support that.

I was not a big fan of President Bill Clinton either, but that didn't mean that I hated white southerners. I didn't like the way he raised taxes in 1993 or the way he tried to have Congress pass Hillary Clinton's health-care bill, which would also have government takeover of health care. However, when President Clinton signed welfare reform into law I supported him. I also supported him when he worked with Newt Gingrich to lower the capital gains tax. If a Republican were to support these failed policies I would be against that Republican as well.

When Rush Limbaugh wants President Obama to fail this is because he believes that his policies will hurt America. Rush Limbaugh has even said that if President Obama followed more of President Reagan's policies he would indeed support him. Rush Limbaugh didn't want President Clinton to succeed, but that doesn't make him a person who hates southern white men, does it? There are plenty of liberals who didn't agree with President Bush and his policies, yet no Republican went on television and said that they were racist or that that they hated Christians for disagreeing with President Bush. Nobody called these critics America haters because they disagreed with President Bush or his policies. Yet we do that to President Obama's critics. Are there some people who disagree with President Obama because he is an African American? Yes, but the super majority of his critics do not feel this way, and President Obama and his supporters need to realize this.

My final thought about this is that it is not racist to disagree with President Obama on his policies, and President Obama's supporters who say that you are racist if you disagree with him are wrong. When disagreeing with President Obama on his policies people are looking at his policies, not his race. This is again showing that America is moving past looking at a person's race in judging them, and this is a good thing. What is bad is when supporters of President Obama look at his critics and make the judgment that their criticism is about his race. By doing this they are hurting America. They need to realize that disagreeing with President Obama's policies is what happens in a free country, and this is fine. Also, instead of attacking President Obama's critics, maybe his supporters should listen to his critics; then they will know what I know—that most of these people are not racist. They disagree with President Obama because they feel that his policies are going to hurt America. Also, if President Obama were white, the same people, including myself, would disagree with the president's policies.

Chapter 13

What the GOP Needs to Do

After losing both the House and the Senate in 2006 and the White House in 2008, Republicans need to go back to the basics, which means going back to the conservative principles that got them elected instead of trying to be moderates or Democrats.

Conservatives could still learn from President Reagan. I know what you are thinking—there is only one President Reagan, and we will never have another. I agree with that, but we can still learn from his example of cutting taxes and spending and having a strong national defense. We can also learn from him when it comes to the war against Islamo-fascism. He was right when he called the Soviet Union an "evil empire." He never backed down from this statement. The liberals hammered on it. They called him a warmonger and said he would start World War III. They called him a cowboy and criticized his diplomacy. But no matter what the liberals called him, he won the cold war.

When conservatives stick to their principles, they win. When they don't, they lose. Look at what happened to President George H. W. Bush. He is a good man. In 1990, he broke his election promise, went along with the Democrats in Congress, and raised taxes so he could end the stalled budget negotiations. In 1992, the Democrats hit him hard on this issue. Because of this, Ross Perot ran as an independent and Governor Bill Clinton was elected president.

In 1996, Senator Bob Dole was the Republican nominee for president. He is also a good man, but he is more of a moderate candidate than a conservative. When he ran, he tried to reach out to the middle. He even suggested having a pro-choice, moderate Republican on the ticket, someone like Pete Wilson, who was then the governor of California. That election year was a disaster for Senator Dole. The GOP was not united, and President Clinton was reelected.

Now look at 2006 and why the Republicans lost both the House and the Senate. Republicans lost because they abandoned their principles. They tried to govern the way that Democrats govern; that is, being for huge government and programs. Also look at 2008. Senator John McCain, another good man, has constantly attacked the conservative base, especially on issues of campaign finance reform, taxes, and immigration. Also, in 2005 he was the leader of the gang of fourteen that compromised with Senate Democrats to allow some of President Bush's judicial nominees but not others to get an up-or-down vote. A lot of 527s (an independent political organization that runs issue-oriented ads against political opponents during an election) didn't run ads for him because he attacked the Swift Boat Veterans in 2004 and said he wanted to ban 527 ads. When Senator McCain was being bipartisan with Senators Kennedy and Feingold and bashing Republicans, the media thought he was a terrific Republican. In fact, the *New York Times* endorsed him in the 2008 primary. But once he got the nomination, he was just another evil Republican. Because of this, Republicans were never fully behind Senator McCain. The only good news from his campaign was Governor Sarah Palin.

Now look at when conservatives stick to their principles. In 1980 and 1984, conservatives were united behind President Reagan. Because of this, he won two landslides. In 1988, George H. W. Bush ran for his first term in office. Conservatives were united, and he beat the liberal governor Michael Dukakis.

Also look at 1994, when conservatives were united behind the Contract with America. Speaker Gingrich united conservatives. Because of this, Republicans won both the House and Senate for the first time in forty years. If Republicans didn't have a platform to run on in 1994, they would have had limited success in the congressional elections that year.

Let's also look at 2000, when President George W. Bush ran for president. Conservatives were united behind him, and he won. Look at what happened in 2002 in an off-year election, when the party controlling the White House usually loses seats in Congress. Conservatives were united, and they gained seats in the House of Representatives and regained control of the Senate. The same thing happened in 2004 when President Bush ran for reelection. Conservatives were united, and they won.

My advice to Republicans in Washington is to stick to conservative principles. When you stick to them, you win. When you try to change what conservatism is, you lose elections. My advice is to listen to the grassroots, not to people in Washington. Republicans should not listen to Republicans in Name Only (RINO); for example, Christine Todd Whitman, Colin Powell, and Bill Weld. Christine Todd Whitman says the GOP must have a bigger tent, which means that we have to become more liberal. She even wrote *It's My Party Too*, which attacked conservative Republicans and said the GOP should be more liberal.

When Republicans listen to this advice, we do not have a clear message in the election. We lose. Why do RINOs always hurt conservative Republicans when they run for political office? In 2001, Bret Schundler was the Republican nominee for governor in New Jersey. If he had won the election, we could have avoided the mess that Governor Jim McGreevey did to the state. Bret Schundler is a good man, but Christine Todd Whitman and the rest of the GOP establishment in New Jersey did not like him. They said he was too conservative to win, so the state GOP did nothing to help him win. It even seemed that some in the state GOP wanted McGreevey to win. So what happened to Bret Schundler? He lost the election.

I am not saying that it was completely the state GOP's fault, but they could have at least helped him out. The acting governor at the time, Donald DiFrancesco, didn't campaign for him. Also, at the one event where Christine Todd Whitman helped campaign for Bret Schundler, the crowd of women yelled, "Go, Bret, go!" She was on stage with a phony smile on her face.

I would like to tell Christine Todd Whitman that President Reagan won two elections by carrying the state of New Jersey. He had a message of lower taxes, strong national defense, and strong leadership. When President Reagan said something, he stood by his words. He never changed his mind on an issue or thought, "I wonder if the Democrats or the media will like me." He stood on principles.

Now let's look at Colin Powell, a RINO. I think he is a hero for his service in the military. But I think he is not a good politician. Colin Powell has again talked about a big-tent GOP. He supports affirmative action. In fact, in 2008, Powell said on *Meet the Press* that he supported Senator Obama in the election, even though he backed Senator McCain when he ran in 2000 and supported him in the 2008 primaries. He was good friends with Senator McCain. One of the reasons why he supported President Obama in the 2008 election was his concern regarding the future of the Supreme Court. Another was because he thought that the Republican Party was going too far to the right.

Look at Governor William Weld, another RINO who supported President Bush in 2004 for reelection. In the 2008 primary, he endorsed Mitt Romney and even campaigned for him in the New Hampshire primary. However, Governor Weld is extremely liberal on social issues and has attacked conservative Republicans.

Why do RINOs always want Republicans to reach out to liberal Democrats and change their stance on issues that are important to them? Why do conservatives have to betray our ideals and values in order to get things done? I don't understand this. Why do Democrats never have to reach across to the Republicans? I get annoyed when RINOs cut the legs out from under Republicans so they can look good.

Meghan McCain is a good person, but she is wrong about the Republican Party. She writes a blog for the liberal site thedailybeast. com. She says she hates extremists on both sides of both political parties. Yet she only singles out Ann Coulter and Republicans. She again does the typical RINO thing. She wants the Republican Party to be more moderate and blames Republicans for not reaching out and being more bipartisan. I would like to tell her:

- "Your dad was a moderate candidate who was bipartisan, and he lost."
- "Why don't you blame liberals who attacked your dad, such as moveon.org, Bill Maher, and others, instead of Republicans?"

One interesting fact is that Meghan McCain only became a Republican when her dad got the Republican nomination.

If nothing gets done, why are Republicans always blamed? Even liberal Republicans always blame Republicans. They never blame Democrats for this. Gridlock is sometimes good. Gridlock stopped the McCain/Kennedy Amnesty Bill, which is a good thing. I am not saying that Republicans should never reach across to the Democrats. If Republicans can get enough Democrats to get a budget passed with tax cuts or obtain increased defense spending so our troops have the best equipment, I am for that. But reaching out to the Democrats just to have bipartisanship is not the way to work. It always backfires on Republicans in the end.

Also, Republicans can reach out to ethnic minorities and other groups by saying that conservative principles are the way to succeed in America. By sticking to your principles and not compromising them, you will win at the ballot box. If Republicans try to reach out to ethnic minorities by becoming more liberal, then they look phony. They lose their message and look disorganized as well. When this happens, they lose.

When Republicans pick a candidate, they should pick the best one who can win the election. They should never pick a candidate just because they feel that it is their time to have the nomination.

Conservatives Ashamed to Be Conservatives/Conservatives Who Always Need Liberals to Like Them

These conservatives are in the media and always criticize the Republican Party for not being more moderate. These conservatives are always praised in the *New York Times* and other liberal circles. One such person is David Brooks, who writes for the *New York Times* and is on the *NewsHour with Jim Lehrer*. He has written about Senators McCain and Lieberman forming a third party. Then, in the summer of 2008, he said that he wished Senator McCain had run a different campaign. Yet, David, Senator McCain is your candidate. You wanted him to run the campaign that he did. If you wanted to blame someone for the way the McCain campaign ran its campaign, blame Senator McCain.

Another conservative is author David Frum, a speechwriter for President George W. Bush. He appears on MSNBC and NBC and attacks conservatives. When he left the White House, he wrote *The Right Man,* where he says that President George W. Bush is a good president, but he attacks Bush as well. Now he has a Web site, newmajority.com, that bashes conservatives. One blog, called "Stop Whining," says that conservatives are whining. He says that Mark Levin whines in *Liberty and Tyranny: A Conservative Manifesto.* I completely disagree with David Frum. Levin's book is excellent, and he doesn't whine at all. In "Enemy of My Enemy," he bashes Governor Sarah Palin and says, "Right-wing conservatives are showing support for affirmative action by supporting Governor Palin." Again, David, you are completely wrong. I like Governor Palin because of what she stands for. Also, it seems to me that David Frum is whining, and I want him to stop whining.

Columnist Peggy Noonan is a member of this group of conservatives who hate conservatives. It is unfortunate to have to include Ms. Noonan in this group, because she has written terrific books about President Reagan. However, she is in this group because she has written praises about Barack Obama and said that he thought when he spoke. She has also viciously attacked Sarah Palin. These attacks are unfounded. For example, in her *Wall Street Journal* article on October 3, 2008, "Palin and Popularism," she writes about the downside of appealing to Joe Six-Pack. However, the criticism of Mrs. Palin doesn't stop there. In another article in the *Wall Street Journal,* on July 9, 2009, called "Farewell to Harms," she attacks Sarah Palin. She says that Palin was bad for the Republicans and the Republic. She also attacks Governor Palin for not being from a middle-class background like she says she is. She continues, saying that Sarah Palin might know who the leaders of Pakistan are, but that doesn't mean that she knows what type of policy to have toward them. She even attacks Sarah Palin's supporters for not seeing this when it comes to her. She says that these criticisms matter because the world is dangerous. She ends the article by saying that America needs the best and the brightest to lead the country. However, she doesn't mention who these people are.

If I ever were to meet Peggy Noonan, I would say to her that she has been in Washington for too long. I would also tell her stop attacking Sarah Palin. Then I would remind her of President Reagan and how the mainstream media criticized him as well. They said he was a cowboy and that he was neither prepared nor experienced. I would also say that when President Reagan ran for president the world was a dangerous place because the Soviets had invaded Afghanistan. It is amazing that Peggy Noonan could forget all the charges that were leveled against President Reagan and now she attacks Sarah Palin for basically the same reason. Peggy Noonan should stop criticizing Sarah Palin and instead start to criticize Congress and the White House for their spending.

I hate to put Bill Krystol in this group, so I won't. But he does deserve some mention. I like him. He helped coauthor a terrific book called *The War over Iraq*. He was one of the very first conservatives on television opposing the appointment of Harriet Miers to the Supreme Court. But he wrote an article in the first issue of the *Weekly Standard* called "President Powell: With Bob Dole Faulting, the General Has a Shot." He said that Colin Powell was the GOP's best shot at winning the White House and that Republicans should support him, despite the fact that he is a more moderate Republican who supports abortion and affirmative action.

In 2000, he wrote an article in the *Weekly Standard* that said that conservatives needed to accept new principles and that Senator McCain was their best shot in 2000. In 2008, Bill Krystol supported Senator McCain again. When he thought Senator McCain's campaign was not doing well, he said he wanted John McCain to fire all of his campaign staff. I would like to say to Bill Krystol, "Senator McCain was the presidential candidate that you wanted to run, and he ran the type of candidate that you wanted."

Also, Bill Krystol wrote "Small Isn't Beautiful," which ran in the *New York Times* on December 12, 2008. He said that Republicans should give up the idea of small government because of popular government programs, such as the prescription drug benefit plan that was added to Medicare. This would be a bad idea because we would then have to change conservatism.

The Republican Party does not need the advice of RINOs or conservatives who are ashamed to be conservatives. We need to go back and become strong conservatives again. We need not be afraid of our own shadow and not be afraid to say to President Obama, "No, we disagree on this piece of legislation. That is why we can't support it." There is nothing wrong with that. Conservatives should not be afraid of what the media and elites think about them if they oppose President Obama on legislation. When it comes to ideas, Republicans need to show alternatives to President Obama's agenda and show that conservatism works for America.

Chapter 14

Governor Sarah Palin

Governor Sarah Palin is a wonderful person. I have a great deal of respect for her. When she first saw something that she didn't like being done in Wasilla, Alaska, she ran for town council. Then she ran for mayor. When the incumbent Republican governor was corrupt, she did what she thought was right and decided to challenge him in a primary for governor. She won the GOP primary and general election. As governor, she has taken on big oil and corruption in Alaska. She has done what she thought was right, despite the consequences. She has a high popularity rating because of her policies.

When she was nominated to be vice president, she gave a terrific speech at the Republican National Convention and then beat Senator Biden in their only debate. She stood up to the liberal attacks. Everyone in the media attacked her just because she wasn't a typical liberal feminist.

But this is not the only reason why I have a great deal of respect for her. In 2008, while she was pregnant with her last child, she found out that the child had Down syndrome. She was given the option of having an abortion. But she and her husband said, "No. We will love this child, and he will be special." Trig was born last year. You can tell, when you see her and the rest of the family with Trig, that they truly love him and that he and all of their children are special.

I also respect her decision to resign as governor before her term is over. She is doing what she feels is right because she does not want to be a lame-duck governor. She is not a quitter. She wants to move on with her life and, if possible, run for higher office. If she does, she has to start to campaign early. It is hard to travel to the lower forty-eight states when you are governor in Alaska. Also, when she leaves Alaska, state business does not get done.

Many politicians have held one office and not finished their terms because they wanted to run for another office. Nobody complained when these politicians were campaigning and not governing.

Name	Office Held (State)	Office Running For	Outcome
John F. Kennedy	Senator (Massachusetts)	President	Won
Bill Clinton	Governor (Arkansas)	President	Won
Barack Obama	Senator (Illinois)	President	Won
George W. Bush	Governor (Texas)	President	Won
Jon Corzine	Senator (New Jersey)	Governor (New Jersey)	Won
John McCain	Senator (Arizona)	President	Lost
John Kerry	Senator (Massachusetts)	President	Lost
John Edwards	Senator (North Carolina)	President/Vice President	Lost
Hillary Clinton	Senator (New York)	President	Lost
William Weld	Governor (Massachusetts)	Senator (Massachusetts)	Lost

Some elected officials leave office before their term is up so they can become a member of a president's administration.

Name	Office Held	Office Appointed To
Rahm Emanuel	Congressman	Chief of Staff
Christine Todd Whitman	Governor	Head of EPA
Kathleen Sabelius	Governor	Health and Human Services Secretary
Tommy Thompson	Governor	Health and Human Services Secretary
Hillary Clinton	Senator (New York)	Secretary of State
John McHugh	Congressman (New York Twenty-third Congressional District)	Secretary of the Army

Whatever Governor Palin decides to do, she is going to do it because she wants to do it. Nobody will force her to do something that she does not want to do, and I respect that.

Chapter 15

Defeat These Congressman

There are nine Republican members of the House of Representatives who need to be defeated next year in the congressional elections. The reason why these representatives need to be defeated is that they don't represent the people in their congressional districts. Instead they represent the elites in Washington DC. The reason why I say that they represent the elites in Washington DC is because these members voted for either the largest tax increase in American history with cap and trade or the biggest government takeover in the economy with the current health-care bill that just passed the House of Representatives.

Cap and Trade

Earlier this year the House of Representatives voted to pass cap and trade. They debated all day on this legislation. The Democrats fought with each during the debate. Democratic representatives switched their stand on the vote. One congressional representative would change their vote to yes and then another would change their vote to no. Many commentators thought that it would come down to the wire. Eventually the House of Representatives voted 219–212 to pass cap and trade thanks to eight Republican votes. If these Republicans had voted no on cap and trade it would have been defeated. The following is a list of the Republican congressional members who voted for cap and trade:

Leonard Lance NJ Seventh Congressional District
Chris Smith NJ Fourth Congressional District
Frank Lo Biondo NJ Second Congressional District
John McHugh NY Twenty-third Congressional District
David Reichert WA Eighth Congressional District
Mary Bono Mack CA Forty-fifth Congressional District
Michael Castle DE Congressional District
Mark Kirk IL Tenth Congressional District

Congressman John McHugh has since resigned from his seat in Congress because President Obama appointed him to be secretary of the army. I will talk about that special election held in the Twenty-third Congressional District in chapter 17.

Health-Care Reform

The Pelosi health-care bill passed the House of Representatives on November 7, 2009. The final vote was 220–215. Thirty-nine blue dog Democrats voted against this bill. However, there was one Republican who voted for this bill. Perhaps if this Republican had voted against the government health-care bill he could have gotten three more blue dog Democrats and this bill could have been defeated. Below is the name of the Republican congressional representative who voted for government-run health care.

Anh Joseph Cao LA Second Congressional District

We need to send a message to these congressional Republicans who voted for either cap and trade or for government-run health care. We need to call their congressional offices and write to them to let them know how disappointed we are in their votes. Also, if you live in any of these congressional districts go to a town hall meeting and question your representative and demand to know why they voted the way they did. Remember when you go to a town hall meeting to act maturely. Also, if they refuse to answer the question, keep pressing on it. If all else fails we should have primaries in these congressional districts next year. These Republican representatives need to know that we will no longer support them just because they are Republican.

My final thought about the representatives who voted for cap and trade or for government-run health care is that we need to teach them a lesson. They need to be held accountable for voting for the largest tax increase in American history or the biggest government takeover of the economy. It doesn't matter if these representatives are Republican. What they did was wrong, and we need to let them know that when you side against the American people you will no longer get a pass just because you are a Republican.

Chapter 16

Idiotic Politicians

Isn't every politician in Washington an idiot? The following politicians really take the cake, though, and they need to be called out. Their actions are going to hurt America and make it less safe in the world.

- **Senate Majority Leader Harry Reid**. "The surge has failed," he said right before the surge in Iraq started in January 2007. What an idiot! This is a slap in the face of our brave men and women in the military. I wonder if Senator Reid would have said this when the invasion of Normandy had just started or the Battle of the Bulge. If he had, the media and every politician in America would have called him out on it. Senator Reid should apologize to our men and women in the military. The surge has brought the violence in Iraq down dramatically. The political situation has improved in Iraq as well.
- **Jimmy Carter**. Not only was he a lousy president, but he is a lousy ex-president. He still wishes he were president. He goes around the world and speaks out against American policies, especially when President Bush was president. When he spoke out against President Bush on the war against Iraq, he won the Nobel Peace Prize. All he did was speak out against President Bush to win it. He goes to countries that hate us and then bashes America. Jimmy Carter should do America a favor and grow peanuts on his farm. Then he could stop going around the world and speaking out against

America. Also, Jimmy Carter goes on *NBC Nightly News* with Brian Williams, and when he is asked about the critics of President Obama, he says that they are racist in their criticism. Jimmy Carter is playing politics with that statement. People can criticize the president and not be racist. People criticized Jimmy Carter when he was president, and he is white. Does that make them racist? No it doesn't.

- **Representative Barney Frank.** In the summer of 2008, he said that there was no problem when asked about Fannie Mae and Freddie Mac. Just recently, he didn't want the Defense of Marriage Act to come before the Supreme Court because his view would lose. He called Associate Antonin Scalia a "homophobe." Barney Frank should go back and tell the truth about Fannie Mae and Freddie Mac. Shame on him for calling Justice Scalia a homophobe because he disagreed with him on gay marriage. He wouldn't like it if someone called him a name because of a disagreement over gay marriage.

- **Representative John Conyers and Senator Patrick Leahy.** They are chairmen of the Judiciary Committees, with Conyers in the House and Leahy in the Senate. They now want truth commissions investigating the Bush administration in dealing with torture and intelligence in the war on terror. This is nothing more than a witch hunt to try to trap people and embarrass those who served this country honorably. If they want a true truth commission about torturing people, then they should investigate President Franklin D. Roosevelt, who attacked Germany in World War II even though Japan attacked us at Pearl Harbor. They should also investigate the fact that he had internment camps with Japanese Americans, some of whom were second- and third-generation citizens. He also had tribunals during World War II. They should also investigate President Harry Truman because he dropped two atomic bombs on Japan. Under the Bush administration, there was no torture. Now President Obama changes the definition of torture, so Congress wants to investigate. So now that something is illegal, they want to go after President Bush even though the same techniques that are illegal now were legal when he was president.

- **Senator Richard Durbin**. In the spring of 2005, he had the audacity to speak on the Senate floor to compare our soldiers to Nazis during World War II for the way they interrogated suspected terrorists. What an idiotic thing to say! This insults our men and women who are bravely defending us to keep our country free and safe.
- **Attorney General Eric Holder**. He said that, when it came to race, America was a country of wimps. I disagree. Look at the challenges that have been met and fought for in the name of race equality. Does he not remember the marches in Selma and the civil rights activists who sacrificed their lives for racial equality in America?
- **Senators Olympia Snowe and Susan Collins**. Instead of supporting Republican principles and opposing President Obama's stimulus package, they decided to do what was in their own interest and support his stimulus package. They sold out their base to be popular with Washington elite.
- **Senator Lindsey Graham** for always attacking the base of the Republican Party.
- **Senators Olympia Snowe, Susan Collins, Bob Bennett, Orrin Hatch, Dick Lugar, and John Voinovich**, who voted to confirm Cass Sunstein as regulatory czar.
- The eight Republicans mentioned in the previous chapter who voted to pass cap and trade.
- The one Republican mentioned in the previous chapter who voted for Pelosi's health-care bill.
- **Representative John Murtha**. He originally supported the war in Iraq. Then the Haditha incident occurred, where he accused our marines, without any proof, of killing innocent civilians. Our soldiers were eventually acquitted. Yet he still has not apologized for his allegations.
- **Representative Henry Waxman**. He recently wrote the cap-and-trade bill, which passed the House. The bill was about a thousand pages long, but he didn't read the bill. If you want a bill to become law, the least you could is to read it.
- **Secretary of Homeland Security Janet Napolitano**. In testimony before the House of Representatives, she barely brought up the war on terror. She does not think that there is a drug war on the border

with Mexico. In testimony before the Senate, she stopped using the term "war on terror." Instead, she called it "a man-made disaster." This statement is completely idiotic. A man-made disaster is an economic disaster. Calling the war on terror a "man-made disaster" is dangerous, and it will cost lives.

- **Senator Arlen Specter**. He puts himself above his country and the GOP. This is why people hate politicians.
- **Vice President Joe Biden**. When asked about higher taxes, he said, "It's patriotic to pay taxes." Can you imagine if former vice president Quayle had made that same remark in 1990 when President Bush went along with the Democrats in Congress to raise taxes? The media would have raked him over the coals. I am patriotic, but I cannot afford to pay higher taxes.
- **Representative Alan Grayson**. While speaking about health-care reform on the House floor, Representative Grayson said that the Republicans' plan was for sick people to die quickly. He also said that Republicans wanted old people to die quickly as well. Then he went on MSNBC on *The Ed Show* and said that FOX News and the Republican collaborators are the enemy of America. They are the enemy of anyone who cares about health care in this country. They are the enemy of anyone who cares about educating their country; the enemy of anyone who cares about energy independence or certainly anyone who wants something good for this country. He also remarked that they are the enemy of peace; there is no doubt about that. They are the enemy. Then on Chris Matthews' MSNBC show *Hardball,* he said that he has trouble listening to Dick Cheney because he has blood that drips from his teeth when he talks. Then he continued, saying that he is just angry that the president doesn't shoot old men in the face. Then he ended by asking whether when Cheney was finished he turned into a bat and flew away. Finally, what is truly outrageous is that he called Linda Robertson a K-Street whore in a radio interview in September. At first he didn't want to apologize, but then his office issued a formal apology. The comments that Representative Alan Grayson made are childish. They show a man who has no class. What is even more shameful is that the media in this country except for FOX News basically ignore these comments. Can you imagine if a Republican

member of the House of Representatives made these comments about a cable news network? Or if they attacked a Democrat who was vice president and then called a lobbyist a K-Street whore? The media would demand that they step down.

- **Speaker of the House Nancy Pelosi and House Majority Leader Steny Hoyer.** On August 10, 2009, they wrote an editorial for *USA Today* in which they said, "People who disagree with the Democrats on health-care reform are un-American." That editorial shows no class. Can you imagine if former Speaker Gingrich wrote an article saying that people against the Contract with America were un-American or if President Bush said that anybody who was against the war on terror was un-American? The media would rake them over the coals, and they would be saying that political dissent is American.

I wish all of the political idiots would just go away. Every time they open their mouths, something stupid comes out that will damage the country.

Chapter 17

The 2009 Elections

On Tuesday November 3, 2009, the people in New Jersey and Virginia—both states that voted for President Obama—voted to elect Republican governors. The 2009 elections were good for Republicans despite the fact that Republicans lost the special election in the Twenty-third Congressional District in New York State.

New Jersey

New Jersey is a Democratic state. In fact, President Obama won the state by fifteen points in 2008. It is also the state that I live in. Incumbent governor John Corzine was defeated by his Republican challenger, former federal prosecutor Christopher Christie. As governor of New Jersey, Governor Corzine raised the sales tax. He also raised income taxes and property taxes as well. He also increased the size of the state government. Also, the state unemployment rate is almost 10 percent. The state had become one of the highest-taxed states in the nation. Chris Christie ran as a conservative who would cut taxes, cut spending, and reform schools.

The race for governor got nasty as Jon Corzine attacked Chris Christie personally, especially in a commercial from the Corzine campaign attacking Chris Christie about his weight. There were two ads from the Corzine campaign that were in poor taste. The first ad was telling women that Chris Christie was going to cut insurance coverage and that he was going get rid of mammograms being insured. This ad was nothing but a low and dirty trick. I especially hated this ad because my mom had breast cancer and was saved because of a mammogram. Chris Christie went on the air saying that he would not cut mammograms from being insured and that his mom had breast cancer and was saved because of a mammogram. But Corzine still tried to attack Chris Christie on this issue, using part of the Christie ad with a woman saying that it was true about Chris Christie. My mom was at a breast cancer walk, and after she finished she did not want to shake hands with Governor Corzine because she had no respect for him because of that ad.

The second ad that was in poor taste from the Corzine campaign was an ad showing Chris Christie getting out of a car, and it focused on his weight. The announcer said that "Christie threw his weight around to get out of a traffic ticket." This ad showed poor judgment and showed that the Corzine campaign would stoop to new lows to win the election by going after an opponent's weight. Chris Christie countered the ad with humor. He called and went on Don Imus's radio show mocking his weight at 525 pounds. He also made fun of his weight by joking that he was going to be the big winner on election day. Then he said that Governor Corzine's ads attacking his weight were helping the economy. Christie said that he was helping the economy by going to IHOP and Dunkin' Donuts and that these people are struggling in this economy and we have to help out everywhere. Then Chris Christie told Governor Corzine to be a man: "If you think that I am fat say to my face that I am fat." I heard him on Don Imus's show and thought he handled himself well.

The Corzine campaign tried to do everything they could to focus more on Chris Christie and less on Governor Corzine and his record as governor. There was a campaign ad that I saw that tried to paint Chris Christie as a Bush lackey as well. I even remember seeing a billboard that had a big picture of Chris Christie's face in black. Then in the upper-right-hand corner it had a picture of President Bush with his right thumb up. In big bold letters it said, "Chris Christie, the same failed Bush policies." I remember seeing a billboard with President Obama speaking and Governor Corzine in the background. The billboard had in white letters "Obama Corzine. Keep it going." I also remember going by a Corzine campaign headquarters where they had signs reading "Obama Corzine for Progress, Peace, and Prosperity." Former president Bill Clinton also visited New Jersey to campaign for Governor Corzine. President Obama had five campaign events for Governor Corzine, and two of them were the Sunday before the election in Camden and Newark. At one of the campaign events President Obama said that he needed Jon Corzine to be reelected as governor of New Jersey. The largest union in the state, the NJEA, was also really pushing for the reelection of Governor Corzine. The NJEA printed up negative flyers and had them distributed in all the public school teachers' lounges. The ads said that Chris Christie doesn't get it when it comes to public school. Another flyer said that Chris Christie called preschool day care. Another said that Chris Christie wanted to get rid of collective bargaining as well. Then there was another flyer that said that Chris Christie wanted to cut teachers' health insurance.

The day of the election the polls showed Chris Christie with a slight lead in the race, but it was still too close to call. I told my friends and family that Chris Christie would win because Governor Corzine had low approval numbers. I also thought that it would be close. This was not the case. As results started to come in Chris Christie had about a seventy thousand vote lead, and throughout the night his lead kept going up. I knew that it looked good when Chris Christie had about a hundred thousand vote lead. Then after 10:00 PM I was watching FOX News when in the election results it showed a check next to Christie's name. I said to my mom, "Look. There's a check next to his name. I think he won." Next Shepard Smith had breaking news saying that Chris Christie had won the election.

The election in New Jersey is not a repudiation of President Obama but is a repudiation of his policies and those of Governor Jon Corzine. The people of New Jersey said that they have had it with higher taxes, bigger government, and deficit spending. The voters said that they want lower taxes and want to stop corruption. In fact, the top three issues of voters were property taxes, income taxes, and corruption. Another thing that helped Chris Christie win is independents. Four years ago they voted for Governor Corzine in big numbers, and last year they voted for President Obama in big numbers in New Jersey. In fact, New Jersey is probably one of the most Democratic states. This year they voted for Chris Christie in big numbers, and he won it by five points, a bigger margin than Governor Whitman won by in 1993.

Virginia

Now let's look at the Commonwealth of Virginia. Virginia has been starting to trend Democratic in recent years. There was the election of Democrat Mark Warner in 2001 to the governorship. Then there was the election of Democrat Tim Kaine to the governorship. Also, Democrat and former secretary of the navy under President Reagan Jim Webb was elected senator in 2006. Finally, former governor Warner was elected senator in 2008. In fact, President Obama won Virginia by seven points. He is the first Democrat running for president to win the state of Virginia since President Johnson in 1964. Also, in Virginia there was no incumbent running for governor, because in the Virginia constitution the governor can only serve for one term. The candidates running for governor were Republican state attorney general Bob McDonnell and Democratic state senator Creigh Deeds. Bob McDonnell ran as a conservative who would cut taxes. Creigh Deeds is also a right-of-center candidate. However, in the endorsement in the *Washington Post* on October 18, 2009, the editorial said that Creigh Deeds was the best candidate and a tax cutter despite wanting to raise the gas tax.

President Obama had endorsed Creigh Deeds in the governor's race in Virginia. He visited Virginia and had a couple of events for Bob McDonnell as well. In fact, he said that "we need to keep Virginia moving in the right direction." However, once it looked as if Virginia was going to go Republican in the governor's race, President Obama stopped visiting. President Obama never visited Virginia as much as he visited New Jersey in the 2009 election. Especially toward the end of the race he kind of kept his distance as the polls kept showing Bob McDonnell with a double-digit lead. In fact, White House press secretary Robert Gibbs said before the election that the vote in Virginia was in no way a referendum on President Obama or his policies. Also, President Obama's political advisor David Axelrod said that Creigh Deeds was losing because he was a bad candidate and that the election would have nothing to do with President Obama or his policies.

When election day came the media said that Virginia was going to elect a Republican governor, probably by ten points. However, nobody thought that it was going to be the huge landslide that it was. Bob McDonnell won the election by nineteen points. He did well all over the state of Virginia, even in the Democratic areas near Washington DC. In fact, on Sean Hannity's show on FOX News Frank Luntz had a focus group that was split equally among Obama and McCain voters. Most voted for McDonnell. They said that the main concern was jobs. Some also said that they were concerned that government spending was important. In fact, the top three state offices in Virginia that election were the governor's office, the lieutenant governor's office, and the attorney general's office, and all went Republican that night and by huge landslides.

New York State Twenty-third Congressional Election

In the Twenty-third Congressional District there was a special election because Congressman John McHugh was appointed secretary of the army. The Democratic Party chairmen of the district nominated Democratic state senator Darrel Aubertine. The Republican was chosen by the Republican county chairmen of the district, and they chose Assemblywoman Diedre Scozzafava. The conservative party candidate was businessman Doug Hoffman. Right away the media was saying that this race had national implications because it was a congressional race. As the candidates' records started to emerge, we began to learn a lot about the Republican candidate, Diedre Scozzafava. She has one of the most liberal voting records in the New York State Assembly. We also learned that she supported President Obama's stimulus package and she supported card check legislation. She was also endorsed by Daily Kos founder Maikos Moulitas. Many conservative Republicans were angered by her nomination to the seat. Instead they decided to support the conservative Republican candidate, Doug Hoffman. Thirty days before the election Doug Hoffman was not well known; however, when conservative Republicans like Geri and Fred Thompson as well as Rush Limbaugh, Mark Levin, and Sarah Palin began to support him his numbers started to rise.

The weekend before the election, knowing that she couldn't win, the Republican, Diedre Scozzafava, withdrew from the race. In withdrawing she said that she would remain a loyal Republican. The next day she endorsed the Democratic candidate, Darrel Aubertine. Many in the mainstream media were saying that the Republican Party has no room for moderates, and they cite the example of Diedre Scozzafava. I would disagree with them, especially in this case. All you need to do is look at the different issues that she supported and the people who endorsed her who were mentioned earlier to know that she is a liberal Republican.

Democrat Darrel Aubertine won the election, Conservative Doug Hoffman finished second, and Diedre Scozzafava finished third. Nancy Pelosi said that the election was good for her because of New York's Twenty-third Congressional District electing a Democrat for the first time in over a hundred years. I disagree with Democrats and the media who say that this election hurts Republicans. Just look at the election results listed below.

Democrat Bill Owens: 61,666; 49.2 percent
Conservative Doug Hoffman: 57,073; 45.2 percent
Republican Dede Scozzafava: 6,976; 5.5 percent

If we look at the vote, the Democrat didn't receive a majority. Also, by not supporting the Republican candidate and supporting the Democratic candidate, Dede Scozzafava took enough votes away from Doug Hoffman to allow a Democrat to win the election. I would say that this election proves something about county chairmen picking the candidate without a convention so the people can vote or not having a primary so people can choose their candidate. I am almost certain that this district will go Republican in 2010 if the Republicans get to hold a primary and can unify around their candidate.

Despite what some Democrats and the media will say about these elections, that Corzine and Deeds ran lousy campaigns and that it was about local issues and had nothing to do with President Obama policies, I would disagree with them. I would also say that this is exactly what happened in 1993 during Bill Clinton's first year in office when New Jersey and Virginia had elections and both Democratic candidates lost their bids to become governor. In Virginia governor-elect Bob McDonnell did just as well as George Allen did, and in New Jersey governor-elect Chris Christie did better than Governor Whitman did.

Also, President Clinton had passed an unpopular budget with tax increases, and he was trying to pass health-care reform as well. Now President Obama has passed an unpopular stimulus plan and is trying to pass a health-care bill that is unpopular as well. These results should be worrisome for Democrats in next year's election. I would especially be worried if I were a blue dog Democrat who represented a district that voted Republican in the last three presidential elections or if I were a U.S. senator from a red state who was up for reelection next year.

PART II

Society

Chapter 18

Whatever Happened to Christmas?

Whatever happened to Christmas? It seems that people are afraid to celebrate it. Some in our society are trying to make it more politically correct by saying "Seasons greetings" or "Happy holidays." It bothers me when I hear those phrases. It's "Merry Christmas" or "Happy Chanukah."

Years ago, Hollywood made Christmas movies likes *Miracle on 34th Street*, *It's a Wonderful Life*, *White Christmas*, and *A Christmas Carol*. These movies celebrated Christmas in a moral way. They showed the human spirit coming through, compassion, and people helping people. I don't care if people don't celebrate Christmas or if someone is an atheist. That is fine. But it has gotten to the point where you cannot even celebrate or mention Christmas. Now Christmas trees are "holiday trees." A Christmas tree is not a religious symbol at all. Are we going to call menorahs "holiday lights"?

Schools have gotten into the political correctness as well. The Christmas break is now a "winter break." Traditional Christmas songs are not sung anymore. When another school's chorus came to the school where I worked for the holiday concert, one of the songs they sang was a made-up Christmas song called "S-A-N-T-A" (to the beat of "YMCA"). They also had violins playing Beethoven. Yet they had no traditional Christmas songs. Before the last song, the director of the chorus told everybody, "I want to wish everybody a nice holiday season." I wanted to yell out, "Merry Christmas and Happy Chanukah."

In my town, just before Christmas the fire department has a Santa Claus riding on a fire truck around town. He throws out lollipops. In years past, the lollipops would be red and have a white middle with either Santa Claus or a Christmas tree on them. Now Santa Claus throws out Charms lollipops. This is getting out of hand. Santa Claus is not a religious symbol.

I can understand when people who didn't celebrate Christmas felt uncomfortable with Christmas always being in their faces. But now it is completely ridiculous. I know these atheists wouldn't like it if we pushed these holidays down their throats. So what makes them think that anybody likes it when they push not celebrating the holidays down our throats?

Chapter 19

Schoolchildren Should Not Be Doing This in School

There is one thing that schoolchildren should never do, and just the fact that they have done it sends chills down my spine. I know what you are thinking—what is it that they are doing that worries you so much? Well I will tell you; it is singing the praises of President Obama. This should never be allowed.

A few months I ago I first saw something that annoyed me and sent a chill down my spine. It was schoolchildren at an elementary school in Burlington NJ. A teacher there was leading children in singing songs praising President Obama. One of the songs started this way "MMM Barack Hussein Obama …," and the song goes on to praise him and talks about how he sees everyone as equal. This song is nothing but indoctrination. As I mentioned in the previous chapter, we are singing made-up Christmas songs in schools because we can't sing real Christmas songs. But now we are singing songs praising President Obama.

I know what you are thinking, that this is a rare incident and isn't going on in other parts of the country. Well think again, because it is. Thanks to bighollywood@breitbart.com, we find out that there are eleven more elementary schools that are singing a song praising Barack Obama. They come from all over the country. This is nothing but outrageous. These songs are indoctrinating our children, and these children should never have been allowed to sing them. Can you imagine if these same children were singing songs praising President George W. Bush? The media would be all over the story, telling everyone that our children are being indoctrinated and that our children should never be singing songs praising a president. But since the students are praising President Barack Obama, most of the mainstream press, such as MSNBC, CNN, the *New York Times,* ABC, and the *Washington Post,* have basically ignored this story. Here is something to think about: children who sang songs praising the leader of their country have come from Communist countries like Cuba, China, or Nazi Germany. That is why these songs send a chill down my spine.

If these students are learning to sing songs praising President Obama, what else are they learning in school? Are they being taught revised American history that shows America as being an arrogant country? Or are they being taught that anyone who disagrees with President Obama is wrong and a racist? Think about it. I know what you are thinking—oh, that isn't happening in our schools. If I would have told you one year ago that schoolchildren would be singing songs praising President Obama you would have thought that I was crazy. Well, it has happened, and these are only the videos that we know about. If the teachers who took the time and energy to teach children these songs took the same time and energy to teach children math, American history, or language arts, these students would be terrific students.

The people that I blame for this are not just the teachers who taught the children the songs they were singing but the school board and the superintendent and the school who probably approved these songs. They need to be held accountable for these actions. It is up to parents to hold them accountable. Parents, ask your children what they are learning and doing in school. If they tell you something that you don't want your children to be doing, such as singing songs praising the president, go to the school principal and ask him or her why they are doing this. If you work and can't talk to the school principal then go to school board meetings and ask what your children are going to be learning in school. If you don't like what they are being taught, demand that the school board change the curriculum. If this doesn't work, write a letter to the editor and call talk radio and call the school out on what they are doing. If they are embarrassed they will begin to feel the heat and they will change the curriculum. If this still won't work, run for the Board of Education in your town.

A child's education is very important. That is why our schools should be for learning and not for indoctrination. It is up to all of us to make sure that our children are never indoctrinated in school. If they are, we must do everything in our power so our children learn in school and are never indoctrinated.

Chapter 20

College Campuses Say They Are Tolerant of Ideas, But Are They?

We are told that college campuses are a place where different ideas are tolerated. I was told this before I went to college. I was also told that there was no censorship on college campuses. This is true if you are a liberal. But this is not true if you are a conservative on a college campus.

Speech on College Campus

America is the greatest country in the world. Just look at what this country has done. Our country has led the fight for freedom in the world. When the Nazis were taking over Europe and the Japanese were taking over Asia, who was there to lead the fight for freedom? It was America. When America liberated these countries, did we conquer them and make them part of America? No. We helped to rebuild these countries and then handed power back to the people of these countries. When a natural disaster happens in the world, what country is the first to help? It is America. The American people are always there.

In America, you can peacefully demonstrate against the government and not have to worry about being thrown in jail. For those people who protest against America by saying that our government is evil or write signs with America spelled "Amerika," you are lucky to be living in America. In China, Cuba, North Korea, or Venezuela, you would be thrown in jail.

Since the attacks on September 11, we have not been attacked. We can thank former president Bush for that, despite his being called a moron and a terrorist himself. He did not give in or give up. He could have restricted the rights of Muslims who are American citizens, or he could have put them into internment camps. We have gone out of our way not to offend Muslim Americans.

Some people have said that the government has gone after political dissent since September 11. I don't see this at all. Nowhere has a newspaper been shut down because of an editorial against the war on terror. Before the war in Iraq started, people used their First Amendment right to protest against the war. I never saw anyone from the government telling people that they could not protest.

It does not matter that you are against the war in Iraq or that you voted against President Bush or President Obama. Everyone has a right to be heard. But there is a point when political dissent can go too far, and that is when political dissent becomes outright hatred toward our country—such as wanting America to lose the war we are fighting—or becomes violent. When America bombed Bosnia in 1999, I was against the bombing because I felt that the European community should have tried to handle the crisis first. But once President Clinton decided to bomb Bosnia, I wanted America to win the fight.

I know America has had our problems in the past with segregation and slavery, but America has ended those problems. We passed the Thirteenth Amendment to the Constitution to end slavery. But America abolished slavery, unlike countries like Sudan. We had trouble with segregation, and it took some time, but the Civil Rights Act was passed to abolish segregation.

Finally, it is time that we stop listening to people who say that America is no longer a great country. I say: "Hogwash! America is still a terrific country. If you work hard, you can and will accomplish anything. America is a place for big dreams. President Reagan said, 'America's best days lie ahead.' I still believe that. Thank you. God bless you, and God bless America."

This speech would probably be booed if it were given on some college campuses. I praise President Bush in my speech. I also praise America as being a great country. I also talk about America leading the world to fight for freedom, and it is a place where, with hard work, you can accomplish what you want. From my point of view, if I were to give a speech bashing America, blaming America for 9/11, or saying that President Bush was Hitler, the elites on college campuses would praise me. I probably would be booed, but that might not be the worst of it. Conservatives like Ann Coulter, Bill Krystol, Pat Buchanan, David Horowitz, and Jim Gilchrest have actually been attacked on college campuses. This is getting ridiculous. People are being attacked because others disagree with what they have to say.

In another outrage, the president of Iran spoke at Columbia University; this is the same man who denies the Holocaust and wants to wipe Israel off the face of the earth. The president of the university gave him a negative introduction, but he still invited this man to speak, and the university rolled out the welcome mat.

When I was a student in college in 1996 and was at a lecture about the recent presidential election, one of the professors said, "The Republicans lost because they had passed testosterone legislation, such as reforming welfare reform."

I asked, "Didn't President Clinton win reelection because he signed welfare or testosterone legislation and he had promised to do this when he first ran?"

Shocked, the professor said, "You're absolutely right."

In the spring of 1997, a feminist professor said that what Neil Armstrong said on the moon ("One small step for man; one giant leap for mankind") was sexist. Then she said that there were no biological differences between men and women.

She said, "Society says there are differences, and society is sexist."

In the fall of 1997, a liberal political science professor said, "Affirmative action is a positive freedom, and we need more affirmative-action programs."

In the fall of 1998, an American history professor said, "Unfortunately, the same clause that was used to impeach Nixon can impeach Clinton."

In a class, we were talking about the results of the congressional elections. The professor was gleefully talking about how great Democrats were. Then we were talking about the upcoming 2000 election, and he said, "There are nitwits out there who still like Dan Quayle and want to see him as president."

In 2004, I was on a college campus and saw stickers posted all around the campus with a photo of President Bush. Under his photo was the word "terrorist." Have you noticed that the people who attack speakers on college campuses are liberal? I have not heard of a conservative attacking a liberal speaker on a college campus. If he or she had, the media would be reporting on it for years. In my opinion, I would say that conservative groups are more tolerant, because you never hear anything bad about a conservative group.

Advice for Parents

- When you pick out a school, ask the administration questions about what type of tolerance they have for different points of view.
- If the college has had trouble when a conservative speaker comes to campus, then imagine what other kinds of trouble they might have as well. Consider sending your child to another college.

Advice for Liberal College Students

- Know that you have every right to disagree with someone. If you truly don't like the person, you don't have to see him or her; but show respect to that person. You wouldn't like it if you were speaking and people called you names or attacked you on stage.
- Have a speaker with opposing viewpoints come on another night.
- Act your age.
- If you disagree with someone, don't attack him or her on stage. When you do this, not only are you being intolerant, but you are acting like a spoiled brat. Would you like it if a conservative attacked a liberal giving a speech on your college campus?

Advice for Conservative Students

- Don't give up. Know that you have a right to your opinion. If you want to bring a conservative speaker to your campus, go ahead. Bring video cameras as well. If liberal student organizations plan to protest the event or want it canceled, call them out on it. Ask them "Why don't you want this speaker to speak?"
- If these groups still want to protest the event, write a letter to the editor or call a talk radio station and tell them what they plan to

do. Hand out flyers with the organization that plans to protest the event. Use exact quotes as well. If they threaten to disrupt the speech, let them know that you wouldn't disrupt their event if they had a liberal speaker. On the day of the speech, make sure there is extra security.

- If things go well and nobody protests, praise the liberal groups on campus for acting maturely and allowing freedom of speech on campus. If your speech is disrupted, call them out on it. Hand out flyers naming the people who disrupted the speech and what organizations they belonged to. Also write to the editor of the local papers saying the same thing. Finally, call a talk radio station and tell them what happened and who was responsible.
- Hang in there. Conservative groups out there, such as Young America's Foundation, are having conservative speech on campuses. David Horowitz writes about this a lot.

Chapter 21

Society Rewarding Bad Behavior

What do Timothy Geithner, Tom Daschle, Bill Richardson, Kathleen Sebelius, and Charlie Rangel have in common? They have all been rewarded for their bad behavior.

- **Treasury Secretary Timothy Geithner**. President Obama chose him to become treasury secretary because he helped to design the original bailout plan. But we soon learned that he had not paid back taxes on the salary of a nanny he had once employed. He eventually paid some of his back taxes, but only after he was nominated. This is a joke because he is now in charge of the IRS.
- **Senator Tom Daschle**. Nominated to be Health and Human Services secretary, he didn't pay back taxes. He eventually did the right thing and withdrew his nomination.
- **New Mexico Governor Bill Richardson**. He was nominated to be commerce secretary until he withdrew his name because he was involved in a pay-to-play scandal.
- **Health and Human Services Secretary Kathleen Sebelius**. When she was nominated, it was discovered that she and her husband owed money in taxes, but they decided to pay what they owed.

Why didn't President Obama withdraw the names of Secretary Geithner and Secretary Sebelius? I am sure there are plenty of people out there who have paid their taxes and agree with President Obama.

By not withdrawing their names, President Obama is sending the wrong message—that actions have no consequences.

- **Representative Charlie Rangel**. He is head of the House Ways and Means Committee, the committee that writes tax law, but he owes taxes on a rental home in the Dominican Republic. He should be removed as chairman. By not doing this again, we are saying that actions have no consequences.

Rewarding these people for their bad behavior sends the wrong message to society. It says that actions don't have consequences, when indeed they do. They must have consequences, and they must continue to have consequences.

I would like to make one final point in this chapter. America has a population of over three hundred million people, and the best people we can find to be treasury secretary, secretary of Health and Human Services, and House Ways and Means Committee chairman are a bunch of tax cheats. This says something bad about our country, considering that the treasury secretary is the head of the IRS and the House Ways and Means Committee writes our tax laws. Isn't there someone in America who agrees with President Obama's economic policy who has paid all of their taxes? Isn't there a person who is as liberal as Charlie Rangel in Congress who has paid their taxes and could do both of these jobs? Again, this is something to think about.

Chapter 22

Levi Johnston, Please Go Away

I don't know about you, but I wish Levi Johnston would just go away. To me it seems that lately he has been on most morning talk shows and *Entertainment Tonight* as well. All it seems he does is bash the Palin family. I wish he would just shut and go away. The only thing that he does is waste time.

As we all know Levi Johnston is the ex-fiancé of Bristol Palin, and together they had a child out of wedlock. They had planned to get married after they both graduated from college; however, for some reason they broke up. Now it seems that the media, which hates Sarah Palin, wants to hear all this supposed dirt about the Palin family. So they decide to go and talk to Levi Johnston. First someone interviews him in his truck, and he says that he misses Bristol and wishes that they could get back together. However, it didn't stop there. In interviews given on such shows as *Good Morning America* and *Today* in New York he goes on to say that he wishes that he could see his son more than he is allowed to and that Mrs. Palin won't allow him to see his son. Then when Governor Palin resigned as Alaska governor the media again trying to expose her as someone who is not what she says she is and said that the reason why Sarah Palin resigned as governor of Alaska "is because of the money."

Levi Johnston isn't done yet. In fact, he is still going on television shows like *Today* in New York and *Good Morning America* and *Entertainment Tonight*. This time he is talking about his being in a photo spread in *Playgirl Magazine.* I remember listening to a segment about him on *Entertainment Tonight.* He was basically attacking Governor Sarah Palin. He went on to say that Sarah Palin and Todd Palin have fights and that they frequently yell at each other. He also said that when Governor Palin was first told of Bristol's being pregnant she yelled that Bristol had ruined her future. Also, the interviewer on the show said, "Do you have any more dirt on the Palins?" and he said that he did. He also said that he would like to tell these supposed dirty secrets and that he wanted to write a book about these secrets. I think the reason why he wants to wait to write this supposed book is because he wants to see if Governor Palin runs for president, and he also needs to think up things that he can tell about Governor Palin and her family.

I have a very low opinion of Levi Johnston. I think that the only reason why he is doing this and doing a spread in *Playgirl* is because he wants to continue to have his fifteen minutes of fame and he wants to have the attention. Also, I believe that he wants to continue to try to embarrass the Palin family, and whether what he says is true or not, the media will listen to him. Does Levi Johnston know that when he goes on these television shows the media is using him to try to embarrass Governor Palin and her family? He sounds like an idiot when he goes on these television shows. I would also like to say that I don't believe a word of what is coming out of Levi Johnston. In fact, this is how much I don't believe Levi Johnston: if I were to meet him and I asked him what I was wearing and he told me I wouldn't believe him.

I have some advice for Levi Johnston, and that is to stop going on television and bashing your son's mom's family. If you really loved your son you would stop doing these interviews. Also, the media is only using you because they feel that by interviewing you they can embarrass Governor Palin and her family. Also, again, if you loved your son you would go and talk to Bristol Palin and her family and ask her to let you be a part of your son's life, and you would try to provide money and love to your son instead of speaking out against Governor Palin and her family. Because every time you go on television it becomes more likely that your son will eventually find out what you said, and when he gets older he will lose respect for you. Also, why don't you try to go to college or a trade school and then try to get a good job and be a good citizen so your son can be proud of you when he gets older?

Chapter 23

Two Ways That Life Has Been Cheapened in America

Terri Schiavo

Terri Schiavo is a woman who was left in a vegetative state because of an accident that happened in 1990. In 2003 her husband wanted to end her life by taking her off her feeding tube. Her parents went to court to stop her husband. Eventually Florida governor Jeb Bush put a temporary stop to this. However in 2005 Schiavo's husband went back to court and said that she would have wanted this. Again her family went to court to keep this from happening. But the courts denied them this request. This time Congress and President Bush tried to step in to stop the husband's decision. A federal court denied them their request. Eventually the feeding tube was removed, and Terry Schiavo died fourteen days later, on March 31, 2005.

In my opinion, what happened to Terri Schiavo was murder. It was nothing but disgraceful. She was a living human being who had family who wanted to take care of her and her husband, and the government said no.

Look at the way they made her die. They pulled out her feeding tube. This is nothing more than torture, plain and simple. We give death row inmates more compassion and respect when we execute them. They get a last meal, and some die by lethal injection. Never mind that the person on death row is there because he or she has been convicted of a crime. If you tried to kill a death row inmate by starvation, you would be arrested and charged with cruel and unusual punishment. Also, terrorists who are caught on the battlefield get better treatment now than what Terri Schiavo got. I don't understand. If you starve a cat or a dog the same way that Terri Schiavo was, you would be arrested and charged with animal cruelty.

I have worked with developmentally delayed students. They are alive, and they deserve to be treated with respect. If the Terri Schiavo saga can happen once, it can happen again. God bless you, Terri Schiavo. I know you are in a better place.

Nadya Suleman

Nadya Suleman has had fourteen children, all by in vitro fertilization, and she does not know who fathered any of her children. Three children of the first six were born with disabilities. We also know that the last eight children weighed less than a pound apiece when they were born. From what the media has reported, she has no job and lives with her mom.

What kind of lives are these children going to have? She has cheapened life in America, plain and simple. People who have more than three children through in vitro fertilization are cheapening life as well. If God wanted women to have three or more children at the same time, it would be done naturally.

She said she likes children. This is no way to show love. If she loves children, why not volunteer with children or donate money to a children's charity?

The doctor who implanted her with all those eggs should lose his job. In vitro fertilization was originally created for people who had a hard time conceiving children on their own. Now it is getting ridiculous. A law should be passed that allows for a woman to be implanted with no more than two eggs at a time.

Chapter 24

Wars Sometimes Have to Be Fought

War is an ugly thing, but it's not the ugliest of things. The decayed and degraded state of moral and patriot feeling which thinks that nothing is worth war is worse. The person who has nothing for which he is willing to fight, nothing which is more important than his own personal safety, is a miserable creature and has no chance of being free unless made and kept so by the exertions of better men than himself.

—John Stuart Mill, English economist and philosopher (1806–1873)

I couldn't agree more. War is ugly. I don't like it when somebody says that another person is pro-war. Nobody is pro-war. War is hell. But you sometimes have to fight wars in order to be free and stop evil. If we don't, our freedoms will be taken away from us and our values will be destroyed.

If we didn't fight the Revolutionary War, the United States would not be a country. If we didn't stand up to the British in the War of 1812, what would have happened to America? If Europe hadn't stood up to Napoleon, what would have happened? If Abraham Lincoln could have reunited the North and South without fighting, he would have done so in order to avoid the death toll. If we hadn't fought Hitler and the Japanese during World War II, Europe would be in the hands of Nazi Germany and this book would be written in German. Most likely, this book wouldn't even be written at all in Hitler's Germany. Also, Japan would be ruling Asia right now.

When we fight a war, we should fight it with everything we have. We should hold nothing back. We shouldn't fight wars the way we fought in Vietnam. When wars are fought, mistakes are made. No war is fought perfectly. After all, the people who plan and fight the battles are human. Look at how many generals President Lincoln went through during the Civil War until he found success with General Grant.

Some are probably thinking right now, "Oh, that is great. You are a chicken hawk because you didn't fight in a war." When I was growing up, I was lucky that I didn't have to fight. I have a great deal of respect for our men and women who fight in the military. I also find it disgusting when they are called baby killers and accused of killing innocent civilians. Some might say, "Would you want your child to fight in a war?" This is a phony question, because we have a civilian army. Also, that is up to my child. If he or she agrees with the war, then I would support him or her.

So the next time some talking head on television goes on about how the war on terror has had mistakes, just remember that this person doesn't know a thing. Remember what I have told you. All wars have had mistakes. It is important to remember the men and women who have made the ultimate sacrifice to help us remain free. They are the ultimate heroes.

Chapter 25

What the War on Terror Should Be Called

I fully support the war on terror. This enemy is committed to destroying America, and they will do anything in their power to do so. When you think about the war on terror, it should be called by a different name, Islamo-fascism. It seems that many terrorists groups don't have anything in common. This is completely wrong. They do have something in common, specifically:

- The first attack on the World Trade Center on February 26, 1993
- The attacks on our barracks in Saudi Arabia on June 26, 1996
- The bombing of both our African embassies in August 1998
- The attack on the USS *Cole* in October 2000
- The attacks on September 11, 2001
- The Madrid train bombings in March 2004
- The attacks on an elementary school in Beslan, Russia, in September 2004
- The attacks on the London subway in July 2005
- The attack on Numai, India, in November 2008
- The attack on Fort Hood in November 2009

Islamo-fascists, people who follow a radical form of Islam, perpetrated all of these attacks. I am not trying to say that all Muslims are terrorists, but Muslims committed all the terrorist acts that I listed. We need to recognize who has attacked America and our allies in the world. We need to look at these groups as the real threat to the world, including al Qaeda, Islamic jihad, and Hamas. Not all Islamo-fascists are Arabs. Look at John Walker Lindh, Richard Reed, José Padilla, and the Chechens who attacked the elementary school in Beslan. But they all converted to Islam. As a country, we must do everything in our power to win the war against Islamo-fascism. We must hold nothing back. The first thing to remember in fighting a politically incorrect war is to recognize who we are fighting this war against.

This war also won't be quick, and it won't be won just on a battlefield. This is a war of ideas as well. We need to halt immigration from countries that are on the state department's list of nations that sponsor terrorism. This is only logical. During World War II, we didn't allow German and Japanese immigrants into the country. Imagine if someone had said that we should allow Germans and Japanese into the country during World War II; that person would have been laughed at.

Let us look at the cultural part of the war. It seems that America is fighting a politically correct cultural war. Anything that deals with Muslims as terrorists is being censored in this country. In *The Sum of All Fears*, the bad guys in the movie were a group of Nazis. In the book, they were a group of Muslim terrorists. In *Angels and Demons*, the bad guy in the book is a Muslim. In the movie, he is white and from Switzerland. During World War II, if Hollywood was going to make a movie, do you think they changed the bad guys from being Germans or Japanese because they didn't want to offend someone? No. Also, suppose that we were fighting a war against radical Christians. Do you think Hollywood would change the bad guys in a movie from being radical Christians to another group of villains? No.

Look at what is happening in Great Britain. They have now banned piggy banks because some radical Muslims were offended. Look at what happened to Geert Wilders, a member of the Dutch Parliament. He was not allowed to enter Great Britain to show his movie *Fitna* because some Muslim member of the House of Lords promised riots if he were allowed to show his movie as originally promised. It is outrageous that a country with freedom of speech would restrict a Dutch member of Parliament because someone might be offended and protest.

Just look at how far Great Britain has fallen. In 1989, Ayatollah Khomeini issued a fatwa against Salman Rushdie because he authored *The Satanic Verses*. Margaret Thatcher stood up to Ayatollah Khomeini and allowed him to speak in Great Britain.

We should not lose the cultural battle in the war against Islamo-fascism. We must not become politically correct and try to hide the fact of who our enemy is. We must not be afraid to defend our freedom and values. If we become politically correct and decide not to fight for our values, we will lose them and the war against Islamo-fascism.

I want to bring up the attacks on Fort Hood that happened in November 2009. The reason why I want to talk about it is that it brings up my two points in the war against Islamo-fascism. That war is being fought on the battlefield and in society as well. This attack was perpetrated by Army Maj. Nidal Malik Hasan before being shipped off to Afghanistan. Even though he wasn't a member of al Qaeda we know that he was a radical Muslim who followed jihad. Nidal Malik Hasan, an Army psychiatrist, was originally stationed at Walter Reed, and then he was transferred because he scored low on an evaluation. Yet they also report that he considered himself a Muslim first and an American second and that he was supposed to ship off to Iraq and Afghanistan and refused to go. Before he pulled off the attacks at Fort Hood he was giving away his belongings. We also have learned that he went to a mosque that two of the 9/11 attackers attended and that the FBI knew that he was trying to contact al Qaeda as well. Also, from eyewitness reports he was yelling Allah Akbar (which means God is great). Yet nothing was done. This is nothing but political correctness run amok. Here is something to think about: during the cold war if there was an American soldier who considered him a Communist first and talked positively about the Soviets and how America was wrong in the cold war and the FBI knew that he was trying to contact the Soviet embassy, do you think that the army would have done something about this soldier? Of course they would have; now why do you think they didn't do anything about him? I think it is because they didn't want to be sued because of a lack of understanding of diversity.

I also want to bring up the way the rest of the mainstream media has reacted. Some have said that there is a fear of a backlash against American Muslims. Some, such as CBS's Bob Shaffer, haven't even mentioned the fact that he was a Muslim. Others, such as *Newsweek*'s Evan Thomas, are more concerned about a Muslim backlash than whether this is a terrorist attack. Chris Matthews said that he contacted al Qaeda. So is that a crime? Then Bob Schaffer again said to Senator Lindsey Graham that this guy was an extreme Muslim so he was part of a small minority. What does that mean? Christianity is the largest religion by far, and they have lunatics in their religion too. All these statements are again nothing but politically correct statements that are hurting this country. I would like to ask Bob Schaffer when the last time was when he heard of a fundamental Baptist who went out on a suicide mission killing people. Then there is Secretary of Homeland Security Janet Napolitano, who when speaking about this event is fearful about a backlash against Muslims. Again now our government is dealing with this attack in a politically correct way instead of looking into how to deal with this attack and not let it happen again and putting policies into effect to prevent another such attack.

I have heard some people say that poverty causes terrorism, because some areas in the Middle East have poverty and terrorism is there. This is simply not true. If poverty caused terrorism, then India, one of the poorest countries in the world, would be a major exporter of terrorism. Countries like Saudi Arabia, a rich country where eleven of the nineteen hijackers of September 11 were from, would have no terrorism. Osama bin Laden is extremely wealthy. Extremists who hate cause terrorism. They preach hate and violence against the enemies, including hurting civilians in order to achieve their directive.

Chapter 26

My Take on FOX News

FOX News is the number one network news program. It has the number one prime-time lineup on cable television. FOX News gets more ratings than the rest of the networks combined. This has made the rest of the networks jealous. So instead of trying to copy the FOX News formula for success they attack FOX News.

They claim that FOX News is a Republican or a right-wing news organization. Robert Greenwald, a left-wing activist, made a documentary called *Outfoxed: Rupert Murdoch's War on Journalism*. The documentary was released through moveon.org, which is a Far Left group. This video was basically an attack on FOX News and claimed that FOX News hosts attacked guests that they disagreed with and that it favored President Bush and people who agreed with him over people who disagreed with him. I can tell you that this is untrue and just a hit piece on FOX News. If Robert Greenwald really wanted to see biased news network he should look to MSNBC, which has only one conservative commentator and has news hosts who get thrills going up their leg every time they hear President Obama speak and always attack conservatives.

I watch FOX News, and it is not a Republican news network at all. FOX News reports the news, and yes they do report in a fair and balanced way. If it were a Republican news outlet then they wouldn't have Geraldo Rivera and he wouldn't have his own show called *Geraldo at Large*. Also, if FOX News were a Republican network Greta Van

Susteren wouldn't have her own show on the network called *On the Record*. Chris Wallace is not a conservative, and he hosts FOX News Sunday. Juan Williams is not a conservative, and he is on FOX News as well. Also, Kirsten Powers, who worked in the Clinton administration, is a FOX News political analyst.

Also, the reason why I watch FOX News is that I get my news without any spin. The news anchors don't talk down to you on FOX News. When you listen to Bill O'Reilly he goes after people of all political parties if he feels that they are hurting the country. Also, conservatives like Sean Hannity and Glenn Beck go after Republicans and Democrats who have abandoned the conservative cause. They also respect their guests. Sean Hannity has a spot on his show called the Great American Panel where he has liberals like Democratic strategist Bob Beckel. Bob Beckel was Walter Mondale's campaign manager in 1984. Glenn Beck and Sean Hannity also have on their shows Pat Goodell, who worked for former president Jimmy Carter. When these guests are on these shows they are treated fairly and respectfully.

Another pertinent point is that if FOX News were a Republican news network why would Carl Cameron, a FOX News correspondent, break the story in 2000 on the Thursday before the election about then-governor George W. Bush being arrested for drunk driving in 1978? Think about it. If they were a Republican network, the story would have been buried until after the 2000 election and might never have seen the light of day.

The reason why CNN, MSNBC, and the rest of the liberal media hate FOX News in my opinion is that they are jealous. FOX News has taken away their monopoly on the news, and they can't get it back. So what do they decide to do instead of trying to copy the success of FOX News? They instead try to attack FOX News as a Republican or right-wing news organization. By doing this they hope they can attack it so much that the public will decide to go back to them and watch the news the way they used to. It amazes me how much the liberal media is trying to destroy FOX News. It also amazes me that they just don't get it. In a way it is kind of funny and sad at the same time. It also seems to me that the more they attack FOX News the more popular it becomes.

Chapter 27

Tea Parties, Town Hall Meetings on Health Care, the 9/12 Project, Antiwar Protesters, and G-20 Protesters

As you know, on April 15, 2009, the American people formed tea parties to protest what is going on in Washington when it comes to the stimulus and health-care plans. Then there is the 9/12 Project, founded by Glenn Beck. Glenn Beck founded the 9/12 Project because he wants Americans to come together the way Americans were on September 12, 2001. This chapter will take a look at both of these projects and how I feel about them.

Tea Parties

The tea parties were protests that were held on April 15, 2009, to protest the out-of-control spending in Washington. Protests took place in many cities in America, including San Antonio, Atlanta, and New York City. These protesters had signs with slogans like "Stop the Spending," "No Socialism," "No Obama Care," just to name a few. The people who showed up were fed up with not being listened to in Washington DC. These people were from all backgrounds. They didn't come to these protests because they are Republican or Democrat. They came because they are Americans and are fed up about what is going on in Washington DC and feel that their voices aren't being heard. They want their government to listen to them because they believe, as I do, that government is for the people and by the people. Now tea party members were not violent in nature. They didn't destroy property, and they weren't arrested. The media called these people fanatics. They have been called racist because they aren't supporting the policies of an African American president, and they have been called Astroturf protesters as well.

Town Hall Meetings

During the summer of 2009 members of Congress went home and decided to hold town hall meetings about health care. They thought that they would get a few people to show up and nothing big would happen. However, they were completely wrong. Instead, lots of people decided to show up and let their members of Congress know how they feel about health care. The people who showed up were senior citizens, the middle-aged, and young people. These people had never shown up to protest something before. The people who showed up to these town hall meeting were not showing up as Republicans or Democrats; they were showing up to these meetings as American citizens who didn't want their health care taken away from them. Some of these people were loud, but then again you can't blame them, because they were going to be affected one way or another by government-run health care. Democratic members of Congress usually acted rudely to these people. Some members of Congress decided to control these meeting by having people write down questions on a piece of paper. The congressional member's staff would select what questions would be answered. However, some of them later decided to cancel their town hall meetings because they didn't want to be embarrassed, or they decided to have a town hall teleconference with certain members of their party that they knew so they wouldn't be embarrassed. Again the press attacked these protesters as Republican protesters. House Speaker Nancy Pelosi called them Astroturf protesters as well, and they were also called violent.

The 9/12 Project

The 9/12 Project was founded by Glenn Beck. The first 9/12 Project meeting was held on March 12, 2009, six months before September 12, on Glenn Beck's television show on FOX News. Before the original March 12 show Glenn Beck asked people to send in photographs of themselves. I was one of these people. On the set of Glenn Beck's television show there is a board that says "we the people," and that board is a collage of the photos people sent in and is made to look like the U.S. Constitution. Glenn Beck also came up with nine principles to follow for being a member of the 9/12 Project. At the first meeting of the 9/12 Project there were many people in his audience and also many who were listening at home. I was one of the people who were listening at home. Many people ask questions, and they also sent in questions from home for Glenn Beck to answer. In fact, because so many people sent in their photos and so many people were asking questions, the computers at FOX News crashed. The people who joined the 9/12 Project didn't join because they are Republican or they are Democrats. They joined because they don't like the direction that America is heading with the government bailouts of industry and the government stimulus. They also joined the 9/12 Project as Americans who wanted to make this country a better place.

The next 9/12 Project was held on September 12, 2009, in Washington DC. Again lots of people showed up to protest that what is going on in Washington stinks, such as the stimulus package, cap and trade, and government-run health care. Again these people showed up not as Republicans or Democrats but as Americans who wanted to be heard by their government. They were mad as hell and weren't going to take all of this government spending. Also, many people had signs and flags. The signs said "No Socialism," "Stop Bush and Obama Stimulus," "Obama is a Socialist." There was also a photo of President Obama as the joker saying "Socialist." Nobody had signs that said "Assassinate Obama" or "Obama is a criminal," and no one had a sign that said "Impeach Obama." The people at the 9/12 Project were peaceful and law-abiding. Nobody at the 9/12 Project was arrested, nor was there any property damage. However, that didn't stop the media and liberals from attacking them. Many liberals said that these people were racist or ignorant. Bill Maher on his HBO show attacked these people as being fat, dumb, and ignorant. He attacked Glenn Beck as well.

Antiwar Protesters

During the Bush administration there were protests by Code Pink, Act Now to Stop War and End Racism (ANSWER), and many other groups that were anticapitalist. These protesters were loud and hateful. I would watch them on C-SPAN because I wanted to learn about what they had to say. Well, talk about hate speech. These people would wave Palestinian flags. They would have signs with Che Guevara on them. They would also have signs that had President Bush dressed as Hitler and said "Bush is like Hitler except Hitler was smart." They also had signs saying "Assassinate Bush" or signs that said "Bush is the world's biggest terrorist." They held signs with pictures of President Bush looking like a terrorist. Yet the media never reported that this was hate speech. Nor did they worry about President Bush's safety. They called these people dissenters.

G-20 Protesters

Whenever the G-20 holds its summit to talk about the global economy many people protest in the city where the summit is being held. When these protesters come to town they can get violent. When they went to Seattle in 1999 there was damage to local businesses, and there were many arrests. Then in 2001 when the G-20 Summit was held in Quebec there was again lots of property damage done by these protesters. They also carried signs saying "Stop the Evils of Corporations" and many others as well. Yet the media never seemed to comment on the violence and the damage that these protesters were doing.

In 2008 at the Republican convention in Minneapolis all of these protesters seemed to converge on the city. Some were anarchists as well. These people threw bottles and rocks at police, and they also destroyed private property. I don't remember the mainstream media complaining about these protesters and the property damage that they were doing.

My final point about these different protests is that the media never really tells the full story about them. When it comes to regular Americans who went to the tea parties or the town halls or the 9/12 Project, members of the media get all up in arms because they disagree with President Obama and his policies. Whenever ANSWER and other protesters get together to protest, especially when President Bush was in office, they never show you the signs that these people hold. And they never show you what the real agendas of these people are. Instead, the media supports them and says that they are exercising their constitutional right to freedom of speech.

Chapter 28

A Movie I Wish Hollywood Would Make about the War on Terror

Hollywood used to make movies that showed our troops as heroes, such as *The Great Escape*, *The Longest Day*, and *The Sands of Iwo Jima*. Some of these movies starred John Wayne, and he was a hero who was always fighting for America. Times have certainly changed. Ever since the Vietnam War, Hollywood seems to be making more and more anti-troop movies that show our troops as being evil and committing war crimes. Now, with the war on terror, Hollywood is making movies that show both our troops and our government policies as evil.

- *Rendition* deals with our government policy in the war on terror. This movie said that our government picks up people for no apparent reason and detains them indefinitely. This movie bombed at the box office.
- *Redacted* shows footage of American soldiers at night going into homes and attacking and killing innocent civilians. It also shows our soldiers raping Iraqi women. This movie portrays American soldiers as the enemy. It also bombed at the box office.
- *Stop-Loss* is about members of the military who have spent time in Iraq. They come home from Iraq and are greeted as heroes. Then the main character is ordered back to Iraq, and he doesn't want to go. He says, "I honored my contract, and I want the army to honor mine." The main character is not a hero, because he refuses orders. This movie also bombed at the box office.

I wish Hollywood would make *Back in Action*, a book by Captain David Rozelle. This book is an excellent read. Captain David Rozelle

99

is injured in Iraq, and he doesn't give up. He eventually trains and becomes the first amputee to return to active duty because he wanted to. He is a true American hero, unlike the main character in *Stop-Loss*. If I were to meet him in person, I'd salute him. I'd shake his hand and buy him a beer. God bless him and his family.

Hollywood could make a movie about another war hero, Michael Monsoor. He fought in the army, and he was always ready for the fight. I heard his story about his military service when Gary Sinise read it during the Republican National Convention. He jumped on a grenade in September 2006, saving people's lives. He posthumously received the Congressional Medal of Honor. Michael Monsoor is another true American hero. God bless him and his family.

Hollywood could also make movies on other topics like the following:

- The many heroes who are at Walter Reed Medical Center
- The doctors who help save the lives of wounded soldiers
- The many battles that Lieutenant Colonel Oliver North has reported about in *War Stories*

War Stories shows our men and women acting bravely to defend our country. These stories would bring in a lot of money, but there is a better chance of Al Gore admitting that he is a fraud and a hypocrite when it comes to global warming than there is of this movie being made. Hollywood will not make a movie showing our soldiers as heroes in the war on terror because they don't want to look pro-war, pro-American, or like supporters of President Bush. So instead of making a movie that people would like and would make money, they will make movies showing our troops in a negative light because they want to give a face to our enemy and show the enemy as being human.

Hollywood has the right to make any movie about our troops. But we Americans have the right not to see their movies. So Hollywood shouldn't complain if nobody sees their movies. The troops they show negatively in the movies are fighting overseas to protect our freedom to make any movie that we want to make.

Chapter 29

What I Would Like to Tell NOW and GLAAD

I get mad when I see certain groups like the National Organization of Women (NOW), Gay and Lesbian Alliance Against Defamation (GLAAD), and others protesting. They have a First Amendment right to protest against this country. But for once I would just like to tell them, "Shut up! You are lucky that you live in America."

NOW

I hate listening to these groups on television saying how bad American women and girls have it in America. I don't like the fact that they still manage to complain about living in America—they always seem to find something to complain about. They are lucky they live in America. If they lived in China, they wouldn't be able to complain about the government. If they tried to complain about the government, they would be in jail.

These groups should look at the way women are treated in the Middle East. They basically have no human rights. If a woman is raped, they kill her. Is this a woman's right? Does NOW remember how women were treated under the Taliban? They couldn't leave the house without a man. When living under the Taliban, when they left the house they had to be fully clothed. They couldn't even go to school.

In Saudi Arabia in January 2002 there was a fire at a girl's dormitory. Firefighters responded, but they wouldn't save the girls in the dorm because the young women were not wearing the proper attire. Fifteen young women died. I wonder if this would have happened if this were a school of young boys. This would never happen in America.

I don't have anything against women. I just want to tell NOW that instead of complaining about women's rights in America they should focus their attention on women's rights around the world and try to help them. Women in this country can do many things, and women's rights have come a long way since Susan B. Anthony. Now women have become governors of states, U.S. senators, Speaker of the House, and secretary of state. If NOW were truly for women's rights, then they would respect a woman who decides to stay home and raise a family just as much as they would respect the rights of a woman who decides to go to work and focus on a career. Why do they mock Governor Sarah Palin?

GLAAD

GLAAD complains about how gays have no rights in America. They say gays are second-class citizens. GLAAD members should be thanking God that they live in America. If you are a homosexual and live in the Middle East, you have no rights. They kill you. Why is GLAAD not complaining about this? I would have more respect if GLAAD and other gay rights groups pursued actions like the following:

- Marched about this particular issue
- Marched in regular clothes with signs that said "We just want to be respected" instead of having outrageous parades where sexual acts are sometimes being simulated and people dress up as drag queens

In America, you don't worry about the government coming to your home and killing you if they find out if you are gay. You can have a bumper sticker that says "Gay Pride" on your car and not have to worry about anybody in the government coming after you. You can live your life the way you want.

I am not antigay. I just want GLAAD and other gay rights groups to realize they are lucky to live in America.

Chapter 30

Why We Need to Always Be on Guard

It has been over seven years since America was attacked on 9/11. We have brought the fight to the enemy. If you would have asked anybody on September 13, 2001, if we would be attacked between then and now, everybody would say, "Of course we will be attacked." The fact that we haven't says that our intelligence agencies have done a good job. But they have also been lucky.

Just because the public doesn't hear about every threat, that doesn't mean that al Qaeda isn't a serious threat. Americans need to keep this in mind when they hear about a terror warning. For every terror threat we hear about, there are many more that we never hear about. But there is something that I worry about, and every other American should also be worried about it. Americans might become complacent in the war on terror. Some people will think we don't need to worry because we haven't been attacked since 2001. That is exactly what the terrorists want us to do.

They have all the time in the world. They can blend into society, and they may take years to plan and pull off an attack. They have to count on the fact that Americans will become tired of the war against Islamo-fascism and want us to stop fighting. They learned this from the Vietnam War. People got sick and tired of that war. We withdrew from South Vietnam, and the North Vietnamese took over. They feel that if we become relaxed, they can use that to their advantage and attack us again. They also feel that if America gets sick and tired of fighting, we will retreat.

Al Qaeda and other terror groups will try to attack us using different types of weapons. They are going to change their target as well. Who knows what kind of an attack they might have planned? They might want to attack a public area in a city, or they might want to attack children. These terrorists see America and our citizens as the enemy, so they will attack civilians as well. This is something we have to be aware of and be on guard against as well.

Chapter 31

Random Thoughts

I wish that some of the elites and politicians in our society would listen to some of the things that I've noticed:

- According to some liberal groups, such as moveon.org, the Huffington Post, and liberal elitists and politicians, President Bush stole the elections in 2000 and 2004. They point to Florida and the fact that his brother was governor and helped him steal the election. Yet President Bush never lost a recount. In 2004, when President Bush won Ohio by more than one hundred thousand votes, they claimed that he cheated in Ohio. HBO made a documentary, *Stealing Democracy*, about the voting machines. The manufacturer said that computer machines could be tampered with. When the Democrats gained control of both the House and the Senate in 2006, nobody on the Far Left complained about people having a hard time voting. When President Obama won the election in 2008, the liberal Left never complained about voting problems after the election. If the Bush administration and Republicans were this powerful, wouldn't they have ensured that the Democrats wouldn't win control of Congress in 2006? Wouldn't they do everything in their power so a Democrat would not be elected president? I want people on the Left to think before they just allege cheating and people being stopped before voting.

- I don't care what the EU and elites of the world think about us as a country. As long as our actions help America, that is what counts. Now if the UN and others hate the way we treat captured terrorists, I don't care, as long as we gain information that can save American lives. That is the main thing that counts. If the world hates Gitmo, who cares? These terrorists are locked away and not killing people. I wish the Left in this country would care about what is in the best interest of America instead of what we can do to be liked in the world. I would rather fight for what is right and protect Americans than have the EU and UN like us.

- I don't understand why if you believe that global warming isn't happening you are called a "flat earther." If you are a scientist who doesn't believe that global warming is happening you are being paid off by the oil companies. Has anyone heard of John Coleman? He is the founder and president of the Weather Channel, and he believes that global warming isn't happening. Also, just because you don't believe that global warming is happening, this doesn't mean that you don't believe in a clean environment. It just means that we can have a clean environment without having more government regulation in our lives and allowing government and private businesses to work together.

- I can't stand how Hollywood celebrities like Sean Penn complain about how bad America is. Yet he goes to meet leaders like Fidel Castro, Hugo Chavez, and Assad of Syria. These three countries have some of the worst records of human rights. If America is as bad as Sean complains it is, he would be in jail and not be allowed to act. Bill Maher said that America is dumb. If he thinks America is dumb, nobody is forcing him to stay here.

- Ward Churchill said nasty things about 9/11 victims. He is the class clown in school who did things so he could get attention. He says all this anti-American stuff just so he can be noticed. Nobody should take him seriously. If America were as bad a country as he says it is there would be no debate on issues, and then he would be in jail and not allowed to declare his anti-American thoughts. Also, if he hates America so much, then he should move out of the country. He could try Cuba or China and see how far he gets by speaking out against those countries' governments. Ward Churchill is dangerous because some people truly believe in what his says.

- Michael Moore claims that he makes documentaries, including *Roger & Me, The Big One, Bowling for Columbine, Fahrenheit 9/11, Sicko,* and *Capitalism: A Love Story.* However, if you want to know the truth about Michael Moore I suggest that you buy the movie *Fahrenhype 9/11,* buy the movie *Michael Moore Hates America,* and buy the book *Michael Moore Is a Big Fat Stupid White Man,* by David Hardy. In these movies and book you will learn the truth about Michael Moore; that in fact he edits his movies to fit his conclusions and will stretch the truth and lie. You will also find out that Michael Moore did not grow up in Flint, Michigan; he grew up in Davidson, Michigan. In his latest movie he says that he hates capitalism, yet that is how he has made all his money. He is nothing but a hypocrite. If he wanted to live by his own words he would work for free or donate all the money he has made to poor people. Also, Michael Moore says that he loves America; however, when he goes oversees he attacks Americans and has called Americans the stupidest people ever. Michael is the type of person who believes what he says, and he wants people to follow his word. However, he never lives by his own words.

- I watched the memorial service for Senator Paul Wellstone. I wanted to offer my respects to him and his family. The Democrats made it into a political rally. Senator Tom Harkin spoke about how he wanted all these liberal things done for Paul. I was angry that this happened. Both Jesse Ventura and Trent Lott were booed at the event. This behavior is an outrage. These two men were paying their respects, and they were booed. I watched Representative Sonny Bono's funeral on television. The service was completely different. It was not a political rally. Speaker Gingrich talked about Representative Bono and how they worked together in Congress. Then Cher spoke about her life with him. No ideology or plan to do something political for Sonny Bono was brought up. I watched the different services for President Reagan. They were not turned into political rallies. At the memorial service in Washington, Lady Thatcher spoke about meeting President Reagan and how he fought the cold war. President Bush spoke about his friendship with President Reagan when he was his vice president and about his leadership. This service did not turn into a political rally. I also watched the funeral service at the Reagan Library where his children spoke. This did not turn into a political rally either. The mainstream media was not outraged when the Wellstone memorial became a political rally. If Sonny Bono's or President Reagan's funeral had become a political rally, the media would be screaming bloody murder. I would have been outraged as well. Memorial services are a time to mourn a person and show respect for the person and the family.

• I have one final point, and that is about the people who led the effort and went undercover to expose the group ACORN (the Association of Community Organizations for Reform Now). Andrew Breitbart, with his Web site biggovernment.com, got Hannah Giles to go undercover as a prostitute with her boyfriend, James O'Keefe, as her pimp. They wanted to expose ACORN as being a corrupt organization. They went undercover saying that they needed to set up a brothel and that they needed to sneak thirteen-year-old girls in from South America. ACORN saw no problem with this, and the pair went to lots of ACORN offices around the country, in Baltimore, Washington DC, New York City, and San Francisco, just to name a few. They were always given advice, and they were never turned away. These people are heroes for exposing such a corrupt organization. They deserve the Pulitzer Prize for the investigative journalism. However, most of the mainstream media has attacked them for their work. ACORN said that they were being set up and just a few bad employees were responsible and that they did not represent the whole organization. Can you imagine if instead of exposing ACORN they had exposed a conservative organization giving them the same advice? The mainstream media would be saying that they did the greatest thing ever in exposing this organization. On a serious note, in Maryland Hannah Giles is being prosecuted by a Democratic district attorney because she taped ACORN employees without their permission. I wonder if this same prosecutor would prosecute if she did this to a conservative organization. I think not. Hannah Giles needs our help; go to www.defendhannah.com. We need to help this

American hero and prove to the liberal establishment that we will not put up with how others are hurting America.

What are Frank Rich, moveon.org, the Huffington Post, Keith Olbermann, MSNBC, David Letterman, Jon Stewart, and the America haters going to do now that President Bush is out of office? They aren't going to criticize President Obama the way they did President Bush. These people must be going crazy with all the free time they have on their hands. I think that if President Obama runs into trouble they will still blame President Bush. Also, if Iran or Osama bin Laden criticizes America, these people on the Left always blame America and say that they wouldn't attack us if we only treated these people nicely.

Here is another thought about Keith Olbermann, the *New York Times*, Frank Rich, the Huffington Post, the Daily Kos, and moveon. org: if President Bush were a dictator the way they portrayed him to be, these people and groups would be in jail and media outlets would be shut down.

Chapter 32

Why America Is the Greatest Country

I know I have written about how things in America are becoming bad and how we are losing our freedom. I have written about them in hopes of stopping this situation from becoming worse. I don't want to lose America. I still want this country to remain free.

America is still the greatest country in the world. This is a country where people have the following advantages:

- New immigrants can become Americans right away.
- People can become rich and successful if they work hard, even if they were born into poverty.
- People can write a letter to the editor and complain about the president as long as they don't threaten him.
- People can write a book about the president, criticize his policies, and say why he hurts America and not have to go into hiding from the government.
- People can protest in front of government buildings and not be arrested as long as they are peaceful.

People should try protesting in China and see how long they can do that before they are arrested. It would be a matter of minutes.

Anybody in America can become famous and successful. A college dropout like Bill Gates helped change the way we use computers. There is some dreamer in a basement or garage who is trying to come up with the next great invention. Don't give up. If you truly believe in yourself, your dreams will come true.

I hate it when people say that we can't have big dreams. America has always had big dreams. The founding fathers had a big dream of breaking away from England. The Wright Brothers had a big dream of flying. We Americans must never stop dreaming big dreams. We must always try to live up to our potential. The day we stop dreaming big is the day the American dream dies.

America is a force for good in the world. When a natural disaster strikes, the world turns to America. Americans are always there to help, whether it be through religious organizations or through volunteer services. Americans are always the ones who fight for what is good in the world. We always lead the fight against evil, whether it be Nazis, Communists, or Islamo-fascists. Americans always fight.

American is not an imperial power. At the end of World War II, we helped to rebuild Europe. When we occupied Japan, we could have made Japan part of America. But we didn't. We helped to rebuild Japan, and we gave that government back to the Japanese people.

I hate it when people say that Americans shouldn't expect to live the way their parents or grandparents did. President Reagan said, "America's best days lie ahead." I truly believe this.

Our Founding Fathers

Our founding fathers were great man. I know the politically correct and elites will say that they were nothing but rich, white men. These men were great men because they knew that they were only men and that they weren't perfect and would make mistakes. Knowing this is what made them great men. Look at when America won the Revolutionary War. George Washington could have become king of America, and he didn't. He stepped down after two terms as president as well, which was the norm until President Franklin D. Roosevelt was elected to four terms.

Look at the way the Constitution was set up. These men knew that problems would happen in the future, and that is why they allowed for amendments. Look at what these men sacrificed. The men who fought in the Revolutionary War sacrificed their livelihood for a cause they believed in. If they failed, they would have been put to death for sure, and their families would also have been punished.

Of course America has had some bad incidents in our history, but overall this country is a good one. We need to teach this about our country as well. Children today aren't taught about American history and patriotism. This is shameful. We must never forget the courage of our founding fathers. If it wasn't for them, we would not be a country today.

Chapter 33

It Is Up to Everyone

It is up to America to change what is happening to this country. If we don't like what is happening we need to let the people in government know that we won't stand for it. The tea parties, the town hall meetings, and the 9/12 Project were just the beginning. We need to keep up the fight. We need to show the government elite that they need to think about the people they represent and not just the people in government.

It is up to all of America to make sure our voices are being heard. Remember that we represent the government and not the other way around. If the government is not listening to us it is up to us to change who is in government. If we don't do anything the elites in government will decide that everything is fine and they can continue to raise taxes and create more government programs and have the government take over more of the economy as well.

It is not hard to get involved in our government. If you see something happening that you don't like, let people know about it. Write a letter to the editor, or you can call in to a radio station and let them know that you don't like what is happening. Let your friends and neighbors in on what is happening so they can help you in leading your opposition as well. The people in government will listen if enough people make their voices heard. Remember that the politicians in government want to be reelected, so they want to be liked as much as possible. Also remember to hold our representatives' feet to the fire when it comes to promises that they have made. If we do this then they will have a harder time breaking their promises. If they happen to have broken their promises, then remind them of it every chance that you get. This is the only way we will get their attention.

I always try to watch what is happening in America because I want this country to continue to be the greatest country on the face of the earth. We need to support the people in government who are trying to make this country a better place. Remember when you disagree with some policy to always act maturely. Use facts and never name-call, because if we name-call we are not taking the high ground.

In conclusion, it is up to all of us to work together to ensure that the government listens to all of us. We need to be alert to what is happening in Washington or in our own states, and if we disagree we need to let the people in government know about it as well. We need to continue to be informed about the issues, and we need to educate our family and friends about what is happening as well.

www.ingramcontent.com/pod-product-compliance
Lightning Source LLC
Chambersburg PA
CBHW020255290526
45784CB00003B/1263